LION BRAND® YARN

JUST**GIFTS**

Also by Lion Brand® Yarn
Lion Brand Yarn: Just Wraps
Lion Brand Yarn: Just Bags
Lion Brand Yarn: Just Hats
Lion Brand Yarn: Just Scarves
Lion Brand Yarn: Just Socks
Lion Brand Yarn: Vintage Styles for Today

LION BRAND® YARN

JUST**GIFTS**

FAVORITE PATTERNS TO KNIT AND CROCHET

EDITED BY SHANNON OKEY

POTTER
CRAFT

NEW YORK

The authors and publisher would like to thank the Craft Yarn
Council of America for providing the yarn weight standards
and accompanying icons used in this book. For more
information, please visit www.YarnStandards.com.

Published in the United States by Potter Craft,
an imprint of the Crown Publishing Group,
a division of Random House, Inc., New York
www.crownpublishing.com
www.pottercraft.com

POTTER CRAFT and CLARKSON N. POTTER are trademarks
and POTTER and colophon are registered trademarks of
Random House, Inc.

Library of Congress Cataloging-in-Publication Data
Just gifts : favorite patterns to knit and crochet /
edited by Shannon Okey. — 1st ed.
        p. cm.
  At head of title: Lion Brand Yarn
  Includes index.
  ISBN 978-0-307-34596-7
  1. Knitting—Patterns. I. Okey, Shannon, 1975- II.
Lion Brand Yarn (Company) III. Title: Lion Brand Yarn.
IV. Title: Lion Brand Yarn just gifts.

  TT825.J866 2007
  746.43'2041—dc22

                                    2007010009

Printed in Mexico

Design by Rebecca Pollock
Photography by Jack Deutsch

Library of Congress Cataloging-in-Publication

ISBN 978-0-307-34596-7

10 9 8 7 6 5 4 3 2 1

First Edition

CONTENTS

INTRODUCTION

Who among us hasn't knit or crocheted something for a loved one? Whether it was your first lumpy scarf attempt (you know your mother wore that only because you made it, right?) or a fancy lace shawl, handmade gifts come from the heart as well as the needles or hooks. They're usually more appreciated than their commercial counterparts because they make the recipient feel extra special. You'll get special bonus points if you make something for another knitter or crocheter—they know just how much time and effort went into making your gift.

Just Gifts is your gift-giving answer for special occasions all year round, like birthdays, housewarmings, and holidays. There are seven chapters in this book, each focusing on a particular technique or type of gift, from children to pets to quick accessories. Like other books in the Lion Brand Yarn *Just* series, this one is brimming with both knit and crochet patterns for a variety of skill levels.

We assume you know the basic knitting skills of knit and purl and the basic crochet skills of single crochet, double crochet, and half double crochet. If you need to learn these basic stitches or refresh your memory, check out online tutorial sites such as the Craft Yarn Council of America's learntoknit.com or learntocrochet.com. You can also ask questions on the Council online forum at craftyarncouncil.com/cyca-forum. Libraries are also great offline resources, featuring many basic how-to-knit books.

This book follows the standards and guidelines established by the Craft Yarn Council of America to help you choose patterns appropriate for your skill level. Each pattern is labeled as beginner, easy, intermediate, or experienced. **Beginner** patterns are suitable for first-time knitters and crocheters, requiring only basic stitch skills. **Easy** patterns call for basic stitches, repetitive pattern work, simple color changes, and simple shaping and finishing. **Intermediate** patterns include a variety of stitches and techniques such as lacework, simple intarsia, and finishing. Projects that use advanced techniques (including short rows, multicolor changes, complex cables or lace patterns), detailed shaping or finishing, or extremely fine-weight yarn are for **experienced** knitters and crocheters. The skill rating for each pattern is listed underneath its title.

KNOW YOUR YARNS

Knowing the qualities of different yarn types can help you create all-new texture combinations in even the most ordinary pattern.

Traditional smooth yarns give excellent stitch definition and are perfect for cables and fancy stitch patterns. They range in weight and fiber content: everything from 100 percent wool to wool blends, high-tech microfibers, and cashmere. Novelty yarns such as faux fur and metallics can be used alone or combined with others to create special effects. You can even make jewelry with them (check out Michele Ritan's fabulous beaded anklets on page 66).

YARN WEIGHTS

Knitters and crocheters can obtain different gauges working with the exact same needles, hooks, and yarn as someone else. Is it any wonder that they also describe yarn weights differently? The Craft Yarn Council of America has established a set of guidelines called the Standard Yarn Weight System to standardize descriptions of yarn thickness. The materials section of each pattern in this book features an icon of a skein of yarn with a number on it. That number corresponds to one of these standards. In this system, the smaller the number, the thinner the yarn. Check the chart on the next page for suggested needle sizes and other information about using each yarn. If your gauge does not match the suggested pattern gauge exactly, try a needle or hook size larger or smaller.

STANDARD YARN WEIGHT SYSTEM

YARN WEIGHT SYMBOL & CATEGORY NAMES	1 SUPER FINE	2 FINE	3 LIGHT	4 MEDIUM	5 BULKY	6 SUPER BULKY
TYPE OF YARNS IN CATEGORY	Sock, Fingering, Baby	Sport, Baby	DK, Light Worsted	Worsted, Afghan, Aran	Chunky, Craft, Rug	Bulky, Roving
KNIT GAUGE RANGE* IN STOCKINETTE STITCH TO 4 INCHES	27–32 sts	23–26 sts	21–24 sts	16–20 sts	12–15 sts	6–11 sts
RECOMMENDED NEEDLE IN METRIC SIZE RANGE	2.25–3.25 mm	3.25–3.75 mm	3.75–4.5 mm	4.5–5.5 mm	5.5–8 mm	8 mm and larger
RECOMMENDED NEEDLE IN U.S. SIZE RANGE	1 to 3	3 to 5	5 to 7	7 to 9	9 to 11	11 and larger
CROCHET GAUGE RANGES* IN SINGLE CROCHET TO 4 INCHES	21–32 sts	16–20 sts	12–17 sts	11–14 sts	8–11 sts	5–9 sts
RECOMMENDED HOOK IN METRIC SIZE RANGE	2.25–3.5 mm	3.5–4.5 mm	4.5–5.5 mm	5.5–6.5 mm	6.5–9 mm	9 mm and larger
RECOMMENDED HOOK IN U.S. SIZE RANGE	B-1 to E-4	E-4 to 7	7 to I-9	I-9 to K-10½	K-10½ to M-13	M-13 and larger

*Guidelines only: The above ranges reflect the most commonly used gauges and needle or hook sizes for specific yarn categories.

FINDING YOUR GAUGE

Determining your personal gauge is often necessary for a pattern. Gauge, sometimes called *tension*, is the number of stitches and rows measured over a number of inches or centimeters of your fabric. Knitters and crocheters can vary in tension even when using the exact same needles or hook. Unless explicitly stated, gauge *does* matter. Take time to check yours before casting on for a project.

To find your gauge, you will need to knit or crochet a swatch in the yarn and stitch listed in the pattern. It needs to be at least 4" x 4" (10 x 10 cm) for maximum accuracy. Using a ruler, but without pressing down on the swatch (which can distort the measurement), count the number of stitches in one 4" width, including half-stitches, if applicable. Repeat on more than one row of stitches, and average the numbers you obtain. This is where having a sizeable gauge swatch comes in handy! If you are not close (within half a stitch) to the pattern's recommended gauge, go up a needle size if your gauge is too small or go down a needle size if it is too big. Take the time to swatch and adjust your needle or hook size accordingly.

NEEDLES AND HOOKS

There are many different types of needles and hooks out there: metal, bamboo, wood, plastic—use whatever you like best! Many sock knitters choose metal double-pointed needles for their sturdiness and ultra-pointy tips (useful when working with fine yarns).

However, your preferences may vary based on the yarn you're using. Some slippery yarns are easier to work on bamboo or wooden needles, for example. If you're having a tough time working a certain yarn, try a different type of needle.

OTHER TOOLS

Each project will list additional tools and notions needed (such as cable needles or stitch markers). For all patterns, however, you should keep scissors, blunt-tipped yarn needles (for weaving in ends), and a tape measure on hand.

SIZING

Gifts are fun to make because you often don't have to be quite as fussy with gauge: Scott the Bear on page 15 is adorable at any size, so if your measurements are off by half an inch, don't worry! And for the felted items, gauge is usually not important at all. You can generally get it to shrink down a little more with effort, even if it was an inch too big to begin with. Gifts are a chance to craft and have fun without stress!

GIFTS FOR KIDS

Gifts for kids often need to be a little more durable than most—or at the very least, easy to clean. You can substitute machine-washable Lion Brand® Wool-Ease® for just about any pattern that calls for yarn of a similar weight—so if teddy or blanket gets dirty, it's simple to get squeaky clean again.

INCREASING AND DECREASING IN KNITTING

The two most common ways of increasing without leaving a hole are the make one increase and knitting in the front and back of a stitch.

To work the make one increase, insert the tip of the left needle from front to back under the strand between your right and left needles (illustration 1-1). Twist this strand (illustration 1-2) by knitting into the back of the stitch.

To knit into the front and back of a stitch, begin by knitting the stitch normally (illustration 2-1). Before you slip it off the left needle, bring the right needle around to the back of the left needle and knit into the back of the stitch (illustration 2-2).

When it comes to keeping track of increases and decreases, safety pins are a knitter or crocheter's best friend. Need to increase on the right side only? When you're making a reversible scarf or working with textured yarn, it can be difficult to tell which side is which. Attach a large safety pin on the right side of the work, and you'll always know where you are. A piece of contrasting yarn will also work in a pinch.

If you need to do a certain number of decreases, don't bother with constant counting and recounting. Set aside the same number of safety pins and attach one to your scarf every time you decrease. When you run out of pins, you're done!

MAKE ONE

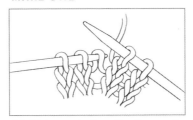

1-1. Make one by inserting the needle into the strand.

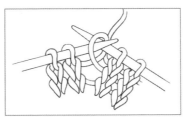

1-2. Knit into the back of the stitch.

KNIT INTO THE FRONT AND BACK OF A STITCH

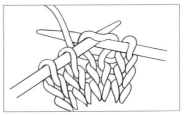

2-1. Knit into the front of the stitch.

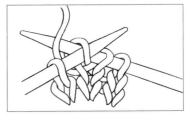

2-2. Leaving the stitch on the needle, knit into the back of the stitch.

INCREASING AND DECREASING IN CROCHET

The ever-popular ripple stitch (sometimes called chevron) uses increases and decreases in a row to produce an undulating fabric. Its zig-zag nature creates a serrated edge and its reversibility makes it perfect for scarves, wraps, and afghans.

Ripple patterns are made in "multiples" that repeat across the row. Often a pattern will be a multiple of a particular number plus some extra stitches. These extra stitches provide balance in the pattern so that your piece will begin and end symmetrically. After you have created the foundation chain, it is advisable to use markers between the multiples as you set up your pattern.

Ripple patterns increase stitches by working more than one stitch in a space and decrease stitches by working two stitches together.

Increase a stitch (shown here in single crochet) by working a stitch into a space and then inserting the hook into the same space (illustration 1-1). Work a second stitch into the same space (illustrations 1-2 and 1-3). On the next row, make single crochets above both stitches.

Decrease a stitch (shown here in single crochet) by pulling up a loop in one space and then a second loop in the next space (illustration 2-1). Place the yarn over the hook and draw through all 3 loops on the hook (illustration 2-2). One stitch is decreased (illustration 2-3).

INCREASING

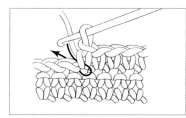

1-1. Work one stitch in a space.

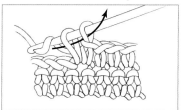

1-2. Make a second stitch in the same space.

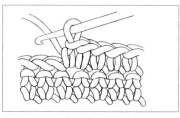

1-3. One stitch is increased.

DECREASING

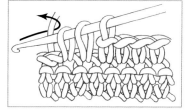

2-1. Pull up a loop in two spaces.

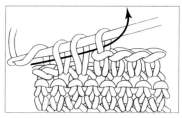

2-2. Place the yarn over the hook and draw through all 3 loops.

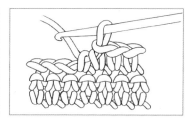

2-3. One stitch is decreased.

1.

FOR THE YOUNG AND THE YOUNG AT HEART

If you're spirited enough to succumb when adventure calls, this chapter has something for you. These quick, fun projects exude a lively sense of style and will have you stitching in no time.

SCOTT THE BEAR

DESIGNED BY KIM PIPER-WERKER
CROCHET/BEGINNER

An homage to the cuddly teddies of our youth, Scott the Bear is a gift you can complete in a couple of hours. Worked entirely in single crochet, this pattern can be used as a launching point for making any creature your imagination can conjure.

SIZE
About 4" tall (10 cm)

MATERIALS

 LION BRAND® LION® WOOL
100% WOOL
3 OZ (85 G) 158 YD (144 M) BALL

1 ball each #125 Cocoa (A) and #140 Rose (B), or colors of your choice

- Size G-6 (4 mm) crochet hook
- Large-eyed, blunt needle
- 2" (8 mm) doll or bear eyes
- 1" (12 mm) bear nose (both available at craft stores in the doll-making department)
- Polyfill or other stuffing material

GAUGE
About 24 single crochet = 4" (10 cm). However, checking gauge is not as critical as ensuring stitches are fairly tight. Consider using a lighter weight yarn and a smaller hook to make smaller dolls, or a bulkier yarn and a larger hook to make bigger dolls.

NOTES
Rounds are not joined but are worked in a spiral. Place a marker in the first stitch of the second round to mark the beginning of the round. Remove the marker when working the first single crochet of each round, and replace it immediately into the stitch you just made.

HEAD
With A, chain 2.
Round 1 (RS) Work 6 single crochet into back loop only of second chain from hook, pull tail to tighten center of ring—6 single crochet.

Round 2 *2 single crochet in next single crochet, placing marker in first stitch of round; repeat from * around—12 single crochet.

Round 3 *Single crochet in next single crochet, 2 single crochet in next single crochet; repeat from * around—18 single crochet.

Round 4 *Single crochet in each of next 2 single crochet, 2 single crochet in next single crochet; repeat from * around—24 single crochet.

Round 5 *Single crochet in each of next 3 single crochet, 2 single crochet in next single crochet; repeat from * around—30 single crochet.

Round 6 *Single crochet in each of next 4 single crochet, 2 single crochet in next single crochet; repeat from * around—36 single crochet.

Round 7 *Single crochet in each of next 5 single crochet, 2 single crochet in next single crochet; repeat from * around—42 single crochet.

Round 8 *Single crochet in each of next 6 single crochet, 2 single crochet in next single crochet; repeat from * around—48 single crochet.

Rounds 9–10 Single crochet in each single crochet around—48 single crochet.

Round 11 *Single crochet 2 together over next 2 single crochet, single crochet in each of next 6 single crochet; repeat from * around—42 single crochet.

Round 12 *Single crochet 2 together over next 2 single crochet, single crochet in each of next 5 single crochet; repeat from * around—36 single crochet.

Round 13 *Single crochet 2 together over next 2 single crochet, single crochet in each of next 4 single crochet; repeat from * around—30 single crochet.

Round 14 *Single crochet 2 together over next 2 single crochet, single crochet in each of next 3 single crochet; repeat from * around—24 single crochet.

Round 15 *Single crochet 2 together over next 2 single crochet, single crochet in each of next 2 single crochet; repeat from * around—18 single crochet.

Round 16 *Single crochet 2 together over next 2 single crochet, single crochet in next single crochet; repeat from * around—12 single crochet.

Slip stitch in next single crochet. Fasten off, leaving a 10" (25 cm) tail.

BODY

With A, chain 2.

Round 1 (RS) Work 6 single crochet in back loop only of second chain from hook, pull tail to tighten center of ring—6 single crochet.

Round 2 *2 single crochet in next single crochet, placing marker in first stitch of round; repeat from * around—12 single crochet.

Round 3 *Single crochet in next single crochet, 2 single crochet in next single crochet; repeat from * around—18 single crochet.

Round 4 *Single crochet in each of next 2 single crochet, 2 single crochet in next single crochet; repeat from * around—24 single crochet.

Round 5 *Single crochet in each of next 3 single crochet, 2 single crochet in next single crochet; repeat from * around—30 single crochet.

Rounds 6–7 Single crochet in each single crochet around—30 single crochet.

Round 8 *Single crochet 2 together over next 2 single crochet, single crochet in each of next 3 single crochet; repeat from * around—24 single crochet.

Rounds 9–10 Single crochet in each single crochet around—24 single crochet.

Round 11 *Single crochet 2 together over next 2 single crochet, single crochet in each of next 2 single crochet; repeat from * around—18 single crochet.

Round 12 Single crochet in each single crochet around—18 single crochet.

Round 13 *Single crochet 2 together over next 2 single crochet, single crochet in next single crochet; repeat from * around—12 single crochet.

Round 14 Single crochet in each single crochet around—12 single crochet.

Slip stitch in next single crochet. Fasten off.

EARS—MAKE 2

With B, chain 2.

Row 1 Work 3 single crochet in back loop only of second chain from hook. Turn—3 single crochet.

Row 2 Chain 1, work 2 single crochet in each single crochet across, changing to A with last stitch. Turn—6 single crochet.

Row 3 Chain 1, single crochet in first single crochet, 2 single crochet in next single crochet, *single crochet in next single crochet, 2 single crochet in next single crochet; repeat from * across—9 single crochet.

Fasten off, leaving an 8" (20.5 cm) tail.

SNOUT

With A, chain 2.

Round 1 (RS) Work 6 single crochet in back loop only of second chain from hook, pull tail to tighten center of ring—6 single crochet.

Round 2 *2 single crochet in next single crochet, placing marker in first stitch of round; repeat from * around—12 single crochet.

Round 3 *Single crochet in each of next 2 single crochet, 2 single crochet in next single crochet; repeat from * around—16 single crochet.

Round 4 Single crochet in each single crochet around—16 single crochet.

Slip stitch in next single crochet. Fasten off, leaving an 8" (20.5 cm) tail.

LEGS—MAKE 2

With B, chain 2.

Round 1 (RS) Work 6 single crochet in back loop only of second chain from hook, pull tail to tighten center of ring—6 single crochet.

Round 2 *2 single crochet in next single crochet, placing marker in first stitch of round; repeat from * around—12 single crochet.

Round 3 Single crochet in each single crochet around, changing to A in last single crochet—12 single crochet.

Rounds 4–5 Single crochet in each single crochet around—12 single crochet.

Round 6 *Single crochet 2 together over next 2 single crochet, single crochet in next single crochet; repeat from * around—8 single crochet.

Rounds 7–8 Single crochet in each single crochet around—8 single crochet.

Slip stitch in next single crochet. Fasten off, leaving a 10" (25 cm) tail.

ARMS—MAKE 2

With B, chain 2.

Round 1 (RS) Work 6 single crochet in back loop only of second chain from hook, pull tail to tighten center of ring—6 single crochet.

Round 2 *2 single crochet in next single crochet, placing marker in first stitch of round; repeat from * around, changing to A with last stitch—12 single crochet.

Round 3 *Single crochet 2 together over next 2 single crochet; repeat from * around—6 single crochet.

Rounds 4–6 Single crochet in each single crochet around—6 single crochet.

Slip stitch in next single crochet. Fasten off, leaving a 10" (25 cm) tail.

TAIL

With A, chain 2.

Round 1 Work 6 single crochet in back loop only of second chain from hook, pull tail to tighten center of ring—6 single crochet.

Round 2 *2 single crochet in next single crochet, placing marker in first stitch of round; repeat from * around—12 single crochet.

Round 3 Single crochet in each single crochet around—12 single crochet.

Round 4 *Single crochet 2 together over next 2 single crochet, single crochet in next single crochet; repeat from * around—8 single crochet.

Slip stitch in next single crochet. Fasten off, leaving a 10" (25 cm) tail.

FINISHING

Stuff the head, body, legs, arms, snout, and tail with polyfill. Lining up the slip stitches of each piece, whip-stitch the head and body together using the long tail from the head, keeping the stitches matched up. Position the legs and arms as desired, and sew them to the body using the long tail of each leg. Sew on the tail so that it helps to prop the bear up in a stable sitting position. Position the snout so that the top is about halfway up the head and shape it so that it's wider across than it is tall, and sew it to the head using the yarn tail. Sew one eye on either side of the snout. Sew the nose onto the snout.

GIRL'S BOLERO

DESIGNED BY JILLIAN MORENO

FOR ACME KNITTING COMPANY

KNIT/EASY

Great for spring, fall, or anytime you need a cuddly warm-up, this bolero is made from an easy-care mohair blend.

SIZE

S (M, L)

Width 13 (14.5, 16.5)" (33 [37, 42] cm)

Length 8½ (10½, 13)" (21.5, [26.5, 33] cm)

MATERIALS

 LION BRAND® ROMANCE
85% ACRYLIC, 15% MOHAIR
8 OZ (224 G) 480 YD (440 M)
BALL

1 ball #193 Leaf, or color of your choice

- Size 9 (5.5 mm) needles, *or size to obtain gauge*
- Stitch holders
- Large-eyed, blunt needle

GAUGE

14 stitches and 18 rows = 4" (10 cm) in stockinette stitch. *Be sure to check your gauge.*

BACK

Cast on 44 (51, 58) stitches.

Work back and forth in stockinette stitch for 3 (5, 6)" (7.5 [12.5, 15] cm). Begin armhole shaping as follows:

Bind off 3 (3, 4) stitches at the beginning of the next 2 rows. Decrease 1 stitch at each edge every other row 2 (3, 4) times—34 (39, 42) stitches remain.

Continue in stockinette stitch until piece measures 8 (10, 12½)" (20 [25, 31.5] cm).

The shoulders are shaped with short rows.

Rows 1–2 Work to last 3 (3, 4) stitches, wrap next stitch, and turn work.

Rows 3–4 Work to last 5 (6, 7) stitches, wrap next stitch, and turn work.

Rows 5–6 Work across rows in stockinette stitch, picking up wraps and working them together with the wrapped stitches.

Row 7 Knit 7 (9, 10) stitches, then slip them to a holder; bind off center 20 (21, 22) stitches; work across remaining 7 (9, 10) stitches, then slip them to a second holder.

LEFT FRONT

Cast on 8 (3, 3) stitches.

Row 1 Knit to last stitch, make 1 stitch, knit last stitch.

Row 2 Purl 1, make 1 stitch, purl to end of row.

Repeat these 2 rows 6 (10, 12) times—22 (25, 29) stitches.

When piece measures 3 (5, 6)" (7.5 [12.5, 15] cm), begin armhole shaping.

Bind off 3 (3, 4) stitches at the beginning of the next right side row—19 (22, 25) stitches.

Purl 1 row.

Next row Knit 1, slip 1, knit 1, pass

the slipped stitch over, knit to end of row.

Repeat these 2 rows once (twice, three times) more—17 (19, 21) stitches.

Purl 1 row.

Work even until piece measures 5 (7, 8½)" (13 [18, 21.5] cm), then shape the neck.

Continuing in stockinette stitch, decrease 1 stitch at neck edge every row 8 (8, 7) times, then decrease every other row 2 (2, 4) times.

Continue in stockinette stitch until piece measures 8 (10, 12½)" (20 [25, 31.5] cm), then shape shoulder.

Row 1 Knit.

Row 2 Purl to last 3 (3, 4) stitches, wrap next stitch, and turn work.

Row 3 Knit.

Row 4 Work to last 5 (6, 7) stitches, wrap next stitch, and turn work.

Row 5 Knit.

Row 6 Purl across all 7 (9, 10) stitches, picking up wraps and purling them together with the wrapped stitches.

Make Right Front the same as Left Front, reversing shaping.

SLEEVES—MAKE 2

Cast on 24 (28, 30) stitches. Working in stockinette stitch, increase 1 stitch at each edge every 5th (4th, 4th) row 6 (1, 6) times, then every 6th row 0 (6, 4) times— 36 (42, 50) stitches.

Work in stockinette stitch until sleeve measures 7½ (9½, 12)" (19 [24, 30] cm), then work sleeve cap.

Bind off 3 (3, 4) stitches at the beginning of the next 2 rows.

Decrease 1 stitch at each edge every other row 2 (3, 4) times, then decrease 1 stitch at each edge every row 4 (2, 6) times.

Bind off 1 (1, 2) stitches at the beginning of the next 4 rows.

Bind off remaining 14 (22, 14) stitches.

FINISHING

Work shoulders together using three-needle bind off. Sew in sleeves. Sew up sides. Weave in ends.

PICOT EDGING

For sleeves, pick up 3 of every 4 stitches on bottom edge of sleeve. Work picot edging as follows:

Row 1 Purl.

Row 2 Bind off 2 stitches, *slip the stitch on right hand needle to left hand needle, cast on 2 stitches using the knitted cast on, bind off 4 stitches; repeat from * to end.

For sweater body, starting with back right edge, pick up 3 of every 4 stitches around entire sweater edge (back, left front, back neck, right front). Work picot edging as above. Block sweater.

FORGET-ME-NOT TEDDY BEAR HAT AND SHOE SET

DESIGNED BY DONNA PEDACI
KNIT AND CROCHET/INTERMEDIATE

This charming set will also fit small newborns—a perfect gift for winter babies.

SIZE

Hat Circumference 13" (33 cm)
Shoe Length 4" (10 cm)
Shoe Width 2" (5 cm)

MATERIALS

 LION BRAND® HOMESPUN® 98% ACRYLIC, 2% POLYESTER 6 OZ (170 G) 185 YD (169 M) SKEIN

1 skein each #379 Cobalt (A) and #372 Sunshine State (B), or colors of your choice

- Size 10 (6 mm) needles, *or size to obtain gauge*
- Size J-10 (6 mm) hook
- Large-eyed, blunt needle

GAUGE

14 stitches and 20 rows = 4" (10 cm) in stockinette stitch.
Be sure to check your gauge.

HAT

With knitting needles and A, cast on 45 stitches.

Work in seed stitch for 4 rows as follows:

Rows 1–4 *Knit 1, purl 1, repeat from * across, end knit 1.

Switch to stockinette stitch (knit 1 row, purl 1 row) until hat measures 4" (10 cm).

Begin decreasing.

Row 1 *Knit 1, knit 2 stitches together; repeat from * across—30 stitches.

Row 2 Purl.

Row 3 *Knit 2 stitches together; repeat from * across—15 stitches.

Row 4 Purl.

Row 5 Change to B and *knit 2 stitches together; repeat from * across, knit 1—8 stitches.

Row 6 Purl.

Break yarn and pull tail through remaining stitches, then secure the tail.

CROCHETED FLOWER EAR FLAPS—MAKE 2

With crochet hook and B, chain 3 stitches and slip stitch into first stitch to create loop.

Round 1 Single crochet 5 stitches into loop.

Round 2 Switch to A and single crochet into each stitch—10 stitches.

Round 3 *Single crochet in next single crochet, chain 3; repeat from * around. Secure last chain stitch into first single crochet to form 10th petal.

Round 4 Work 4 double crochets into each 3-stitch chain.

Break yarn and secure end.

FINISHING

Sew seam on hat. (Seam is at the back of hat.)
Secure 1 flower to each side of hat to create earflaps.

SHOES—MAKE 2

The shoes are knitted side to side, starting with the sole.

SOLE

With knitting needles and A, cast on 10 stitches.
Row 1 Knit across, increasing 1 stitch at each end.
Row 2 Purl.
Repeat these 2 rows once more, then repeat row 1 again—16 stitches.
Work 2 rows even.
Row 8 Purl across, decreasing 1 stitch at each end.
Row 9 Knit.
Repeat these 2 rows once more, then repeat row 8 again—10 stitches.

UPPER

Row 13 Cast on 4 stitches, using knitted cast-on, then knit across all—14 stitches.
Row 14 Increase 1 stitch at the beginning of row, purl across.
Row 15 Knit.
Rows 16–20 Repeat rows 14 and 15 twice, then row 14 once more—18 stitches.
Row 21 Bind off 8 stitches, knit to end of row.
Row 22 Increase 1 stitch at the beginning of row, purl across.
Row 23 Knit—11 stitches.
Rows 24–29 Work 6 rows in stockinette stitch.
Row 30 Decrease 1 stitch at the beginning of row, purl across.
Row 31 Cast on 8 stitches using knitted cast-on, then knit across—18 stitches.
Row 32 Decrease 1 stitch at the beginning of row, purl across.
Row 33 Knit.
Repeat rows 32 and 33 twice more, then row 32 once more—14 stitches.
Bind off.

FLOWERS—MAKE 2

With B and crochet hook, chain 3, then chain into first stitch to make a loop.
Round 1 Single crochet 5 stitches into the center loop.
Round 2 Single crochet 2 into each stitch—10 stitches.
Round 3 Switch to A and *single crochet into next single crochet, chain 3; repeat from * across. Use a slip stitch to attach the 10th petal and complete the flower.

FINISHING

Stitch back seam and sole.
Attach a flower to the top of each shoe.

BRAIDED SHORTIE SCARF

DESIGNED BY SHANNON OKEY
KNIT/BEGINNER

Why tubes? And why is this scarf so short (only about 4 to 5 feet, depending on how tightly you braid it)? Because tubes trap warm air around your neck like your very own mini-heater, keeping you super-warm on even the coldest of days. Wrap it around your neck and tuck the ends into the front of your jacket—it's not terribly bulky, but it's very effective.

SIZE
Approximately 5" wide by 43" long (12 cm x 107.5 cm)

MATERIALS
 LION BRAND® LION® WOOL
100% WOOL
3 OZ (85 G) 158 YD (144 M) BALL

3 balls #140 Rose, or color of your choice

- Size 8 (5 mm) knitting needles (can be short circular or double-pointed needles)
- Size 8 (5 mm) straight needles
- Waste yarn
- Several safety pins
- Large-eyed, blunt needle

GAUGE
Gauge is not critical to this project.

SCARF
Pull out several yards of yarn and cut; reserve for finishing at the end. Cast on 22 stitches provisionally and join in the round.
Knit tube until almost to the end of the ball and place remaining stitches on waste yarn
Repeat 3 times—3 tubes.

FINISHING
Pin provisional cast-on ends of tubes together and braid loosely. Pin pieces together occasionally to keep them from unbraiding.
At the waste yarn/loose stitches end, pull out excess knit rows from tubes as needed to even up the ends.
Place open edges of each tube onto a straight needle by picking up a stitch from the front side of the tube, then the back, then the front, etc., working from right to left across all three tubes.
Bind off.
Pull out provisional cast-on and repeat, placing stitches onto straight needle and binding off.
Tack braided sections together in several locations with leftover yarn and a large-eyed, blunt needle to prevent the braid from unraveling. (It will unravel if left untacked, even though ends are bound off.)
If you wish, you may add fringe.

2.
ON THE HOME FRONT

The knit and crochet projects in this chapter make excellent housewarming gifts . . . or will brighten your own home! From a dishcloth that will cheer up any kitchen to a colorful throw that will anchor the rest of your living room décor, options abound.

THROW PILLOW

DESIGNED BY JOANNE SEIFF
KNIT/BEGINNER

Let your yarn do the work! Knit a slightly off-kilter pattern of knit and purl rows that shows off texture as well as color. You don't need buttonholes to make this pretty scalloped back closure, which makes the pillow cover easy to take off and wash. This is an ideal gift for a housewarming or a couple's new household together.

SIZE
16" (40 cm) square pillow

MATERIALS
 LION BRAND® HOMESPUN®
98% ACRYLIC, 2% POLYESTER
6 OZ (170 G) 185 YD (169 M)
SKEIN

2 skeins #322 Baroque, or color of your choice

- Size 10 (6 mm) needles, *or size to obtain gauge*
- 16" (40 cm) pillow form
- Six ¾" (20 mm) buttons
- Six ⅜" (9 mm) buttons
- Large-eyed, blunt needle
- Matching needle and sewing thread

GAUGE
12 stitches and 20 rows = 4" (10 cm) in stockinette stitch.
Be sure to check your gauge.

BUMPY STITCH PATTERN
Row 1 (RS) Knit.
Row 2 (WS) Purl.
Rows 3–5 Knit.
Row 6 Purl.
Row 7 Knit.
Row 8 Purl.
Rows 9–12 Knit.

NOTE
Slip the last stitch of each row purlwise with yarn in front to create a neat edge.

PILLOW

Cast on 48 stitches.

Knit 2 rows to form garter stitch edge.

Beginning with a purl row on the wrong side, work even in stockinette stitch for 7" (18 cm), ending with a knit row.

With wrong side facing, knit 1 row to create a turning ridge for the side seam of the pillow.

Working in Bumpy Stitch Pattern, repeat the 12 rows 6 times, or until pillow front measures 17" (43 cm) and the entire knitted work measures 24" (61 cm).

In stockinette stitch, work even for 11" (28 cm), measuring from the last garter stitch ridge on the pillow front. The total knitted piece will measure 35" (88.5 cm).

With the wrong side facing, knit 1 row to create garter stitch edge. Bind off.

FINISHING

Use matching thread and sewing needle to sew the buttons to the pillow cover. Sew the buttons, evenly spaced, 2" (5 cm) from the cast-on edge on the 7" (18 cm) stockinette flap. Sew the ¾" (2 cm) buttons to the knit side of the flap, but anchor them in place by sewing the ⅜" (9 mm) buttons behind them on the wrong side (purl side) of the flap.

Fold the pillow like an envelope, overlapping the two stockinette portions by 1" (2.5 cm) with the longer piece on top. Seam the two edges, but leave the slit across the middle open.

Insert the pillow form and close the pillow back by gently stretching the knitting just under the garter stitch edging to form buttonholes. This creates a decorative scalloped edge when the pillow is buttoned up.

BOBBLETTE DISHCLOTH

DESIGNED BY CHRISSY GARDINER

KNIT/EASY

You can never have too many washcloths, and this one's covered with gentle face-scrubbing bobbles.

SIZE

8" x 8" (20.5 x 20.5 cm)

MATERIALS

 LION BRAND® LION® COTTON
100% COTTON
5 OZ (140 G) 236 YD (212 M) BALL

1 ball#157 Sunflower

- Size 7 (4.5 mm) straight needles, or size to obtain gauge
- Large-eyed, blunt needle

GAUGE

18 stitches and 24 rows = 4" (10 cm) in stockinette stitch.

20 stitches and 21 rows = 4" (10 cm) in bobblette stitch pattern. *Gauge is not critical for this project.*

BOBBLETTE STITCH PATTERN

(multiple of 4 stitches + 10)

Row 1 (WS) Knit 5, *(knit 1, purl 1, knit 1 in one stitch) in next stitch, purl 3 together; repeat from * to last 5 stitches, knit 5.

Row 2 Knit 4, loosely purl to last 4 stitches, knit 4.

Row 3 Knit 5, *purl 3 together, make 3 stitches in the next stitch (knit 1, purl 1, knit 1 in one stitch); repeat from * to last 5 stitches, knit 5.

Row 4 Knit 4, loosely purl to last 4 stitches, knit 4.

DISHCLOTH

Cast on 38 stitches.
Knit 5 rows.
Work rows 1–4 of bobblette stitch pattern a total of 9 times or approximately 7.5" (19 cm) from bottom edge.
Knit 5 rows.
Bind off.

FINISHING

Weave in ends and block lightly.

BLUE BANANA DISHCLOTH

DESIGNED BY CHRISSY GARDINER
KNIT/EASY

Dishcloths are an excellent small project to practice slip stitch patterns, as seen here. Slip stitch patterns also add a lovely texture to face cloths.

SIZE
Approximately 8" x 8" (20.5 x 20.5 cm)

MATERIALS

 LION BRAND® LION® COTTON
100% COTTON
5 OZ (140 G) 236 YD (212 M) BALL

1 ball each #158 Banana (A) and #148 Turquoise (B), or colors of your choice

- Size 7 (4.5 mm) straight needles, *or size to obtain gauge*
- Large-eyed, blunt needle

GAUGE
5 stitches and 6 rows = 1" (2.5 cm) in stockinette stitch.
Gauge is not critical for this project.

CHECK PATTERN
(multiple of 2 stitches + 5):
Row 1 (RS) Using A, knit.
Row 2 Knit.
Row 3 Using B, knit 3, *slip 1, knit 1; repeat from * to last 2 stitches, knit 2.
Row 4 Knit 3, *yarn forward, slip 1, yarn back, knit 1; repeat from * to last 2 stitches, knit 2.
Rows 5–6 Using A, knit.
Row 7 Using B, knit 2, *slip 1, knit 1; repeat from * to last stitch, knit 1.
Row 8 Knit 2, *yarn forward, slip 1, yarn back, knit 1; repeat from * to last stitch, knit 1.

DISHCLOTH
Cast on 35 stitches.
Work Check Pattern rows 1–8 until piece measures approximately 8" (20.5 cm) from bottom edge, ending with row 6.
Bind off.

FINISHING
Weave in ends and block lightly.

CORNMEAL CABLE DISHCLOTH

DESIGNED BY CHRISSY GARDINER

KNIT/INTERMEDIATE

Never cabled before? Read the directions on page 38, then try a small project like a dishcloth, and you'll be rearranging your stitches in no time!

SIZE
8" x 8" (20.5 x 20.5 cm)

MATERIALS

 LION BRAND® LION® COTTON
100% COTTON
4 OZ (113 G) 189 YD (170 M) BALL

1 ball #257 Cornmeal

- Size 7 (4.5 mm) straight needles, or size to obtain gauge
- Cable needle
- Large-eyed, blunt needle

GAUGE
5 stitches and 6 rows = 1" (2.5 cm) in stockinette stitch.
Gauge is not critical for this project.

STITCH EXPLANATIONS

C4F (Cable 4 Stitches Forward)
Place the next 2 stitches on a cable needle and hold in **front** of your work, knit the next 2 stitches, then knit the 2 stitches held on the cable needle.

C4B (Cable 4 Stitches Backward)
Place the next 2 stitches on a cable needle and hold in **back** of your work, knit the next 2 stitches, then knit the 2 stitches held on the cable needle.

WOVEN CABLE PATTERN
(multiple of 4 stitches)

Row 1 (RS) Knit 4, *C4F; repeat from * to last 4 stitches, knit 4.

Row 2 Knit 4, purl to last 4 stitches, knit 4.

Row 3 Knit 6, *C4B; repeat from * to last 6 stitches, knit 6.

Row 4 Knit 4, purl to last 4 stitches, knit 4.

DISHCLOTH
Cast on 36 stitches.
Knit 5 rows, increasing 8 stitches evenly across 5th row—44 stitches.
Work Woven Cable Pattern rows 1–4 until work measures approximately 7.5" (19 cm) from bottom edge, ending with row 3.
Knit 5 rows, decreasing 8 stitches evenly across first row worked—36 stitches.
Bind off.

FINISHING
Weave in ends and block lightly.

HOW TO KNIT CABLES

The first step in knitting a cable is slipping the required number of stitches as if to purl on to the cable needle. The pattern will tell you to hold the cable needle to the front (illustration 1-1) or back (illustration 2-1) of your knitting. Holding stitches to the front slants the cable to the left (illustration 1-4) and holding stitches to the back slants the cable to the right (illustration 2-4).

The next step is to knit the stitches that remain on your needle (illustrations 1-2 and 2-2). Your pattern will tell you how many stitches to work.

The last step is to work the stitches on the cable needle (illustrations 1-3 and 2-3). Some knitters like to put them back on the left needle and knit them from there. Other knitters prefer to knit them directly from the cable needle. Try both ways and see which method is most comfortable for you. Just be sure not to twist the stitches as you knit them.

HOLDING STITCHES TO THE FRONT

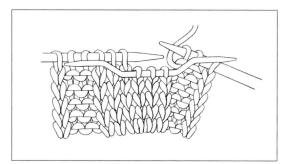

1-1. Hold stitches on a cable needle in front of work.

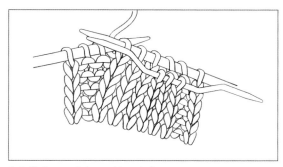

1-2. Knit remaining cable stitches.

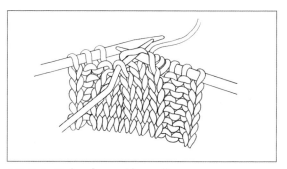

1-3. Knit stitches from cable needle.

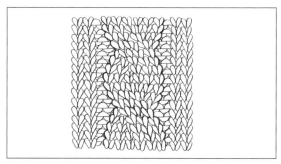

1-4. Finished front (left) cable.

HOLDING STITCHES TO THE BACK

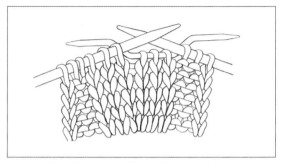

2-1. Hold stitches on a cable needle in back of work.

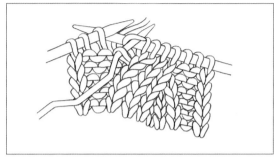

2-3. Knit stitches from cable needle.

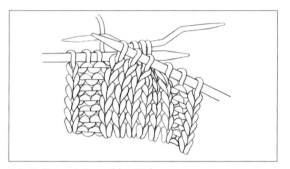

2-2. Knit remaining cable stitches.

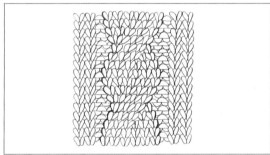

2-4. Finished back (right) cable.

MAKING A GRANNY SQUARE

Forming a ring is the first step. Chain as many stitches as the pattern dictates, insert the hook into the first chain above the slip knot (illustration 1), yarn over the hook, and pull through the first chain and the chain on the hook (illustration 2).

Working into the ring (or under the chain): After you have created the ring, chain 3 chains if you are using double crochet, yarn over and insert the hook under the ring, yarn over and pull up a stitch. When you are working your third or larger rounds, make sure you insert your hook completely underneath the chain below it (illustration 3).

A handy tip when you begin each round is to hold the tail yarn on top of the chain you are crocheting into and crochet the tail so that it is tucked into the chain. This secures the tails as you work, making it easier to weave them later. It is a good idea to weave in the yarn tails as you go so you won't be faced with dozens of ends to weave when you have finished your project and are anxious to show it off.

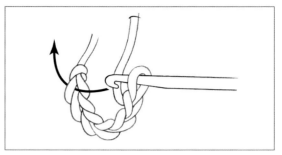

1. Joining granny square ring: insert hook into first chain stitch.

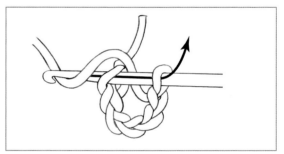

2. Yarn over, pull through chain and stitch on hook.

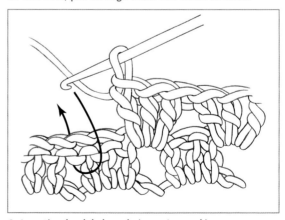

3. Inserting hook below chain you're working on.

PROVENÇAL AFGHAN

DESIGNED BY DORIS CHAN

CROCHET/EASY

The beloved granny square afghan gets a stunning makeover with this half-sized throw, inspired by the brilliant colors of a Provençal-style rug. While traditional Provençal fabric calls for ornate floral motifs, this afghan is crocheted using just three different easy squares that create a floral impression.

SIZE

36" wide x 48" long (91.5 x 122 cm)
Each square motif is 6" x 6" (15 x 15 cm).

MATERIALS

 LION BRAND® LION® WOOL-EASE®
80% ACRYLIC, 20% WOOL
3 OZ (85 G) 197 YD (180 M) BALL

4 balls #102 Ranch Red (A), 2 balls #157 Pastel Yellow (B), 2 balls #117 Colonial Blue (C), 1 ball #171 Gold (D), 1 ball #116 Delft (E), and 1 ball #176 Spring Green (F), or colors of your choice

• Size J-10 (6 mm) crochet hook, *or size to obtain gauge*
• Split ring markers or scraps of yarn for markers (if needed)
• Large-eyed, blunt needle

GAUGE

7 rows of border = 3" (7.5 cm)
Be sure to check your gauge.

STITCH EXPLANATIONS

Double crochet 2 together Yarn over, insert hook in stitch or space, yarn over and draw up a loop, yarn over and draw through 2 loops on hook, yarn over, insert hook in same stitch or space, yarn over and draw up a loop, yarn over and draw through 2 loops on hook, yarn over and draw through all three loops on hook.

Treble crochet 2 together Yarn over twice, insert hook into stitch or space, yarn over and draw up a loop, (yarn over and draw through two loops on hook) twice, (yarn over and draw through two loops on hook) twice, yarn over and draw through all three loops on hook.

Cluster Yarn over, insert hook into stitch or space, yarn over and draw up a loop, yarn over and draw through 2 loops on hook, (yarn over, insert hook in same stitch or space, yarn over and draw up a loop, yarn over and draw through 2 loops on hook) twice, yarn over and draw through all four loops on hook.

Shell Work 3 double crochet in same stitch.

Single crochet through back loop Single crochet inserting hook through back loop only of next single crochet.

AFGHAN

Afghan is made using three square motifs. Each has a different center but the same last 2 rounds. Work squares in joined rounds with right side always facing.

SQUARE #1—MAKE 11

With D, chain 8. Join with slip stitch in first chain to form ring.

Round 1 (RS) Chain 3, treble crochet into ring, [chain 2, treble crochet 2 together] 11 times into ring, chain 2. Join with slip stitch in first treble crochet. Fasten off—12 chain 2-spaces.

Round 2 With B, join with slip stitch in any chain 2-space, chain 2, double crochet 2 together in same space, [chain 3, cluster in next chain 2-space] 11 times, chain 3. Join with slip stitch in beginning 2-double crochet cluster. Fasten off—12 chain-spaces.

Round 3 With A, join with slip stitch in any chain 3-space, (chain 2, double crochet 2 together, chain 2, cluster) in same space, *chain 3, skip next chain 3-space, single crochet in next cluster, chain 3, skip next chain 3-space, [cluster, chain 2, cluster, chain 4, cluster, chain 2, cluster] in next chain 3-space; repeat from * 2 more times, chain 3, skip next chain 3-space, single crochet in next cluster, chain 3, skip next chain 3-space, [cluster, chain 2, cluster] in beginning chain 3-space, chain 1, double crochet in top of beginning 2-double crochet cluster.

Round 4 Chain 1, 3 single crochet in beginning double crochet chain-space, *3 single crochet in each of next 4 chain-spaces, 5 single crochet in next corner chain-4 space; repeat from * 3 more times, ending 2 single crochet in beginning chain-space. Join with slip stitch in first single crochet. Fasten off, leaving 18" (46 cm) tail for sewing—68 single crochet.

SQUARE #2—MAKE 12

With C, chain 4. Join with slip stitch in first chain to form ring.

Round 1 Chain 1, 8 single crochet in ring. Join with slip stitch in first single crochet. Fasten off—8 single crochet.

Round 2 With E, join with slip stitch in any single crochet, chain 2, double crochet 2 together in same single crochet, [chain 3, cluster in next single crochet] 7 times, chain 3. Join with slip stitch in beginning 2-double crochet cluster. Fasten off—8 clusters.

Round 3 With D, join in top of any cluster, chain 2, double crochet in same stitch, *[double crochet 2 together, chain 5, double crochet 2 together] in top of next cluster; repeat from * 6 more times, double crochet 2 together in same cluster as beginning, chain 5. Join with slip stitch in first double crochet. Fasten off—8 chain 5-spaces.

Round 4 With A, join with slip stitch in any chain 5-space, (chain 2, double crochet 2 together, chain 2, cluster) in same space, *chain 3, single crochet in next chain 5-space, chain 3, [cluster, chain 2, cluster, chain 4, cluster, chain 2, cluster] in next chain 5-space; repeat from * 3 more times, ending (cluster, chain 2, cluster) in beginning chain 5-space, chain 1, double crochet in top of beginning 2-double crochet cluster. Fasten off.

Round 5 Same as Square 1 round 4.

SQUARE #3—MAKE 12

With B, chain 4. Join with slip stitch in first chain to form ring.

Round 1 Chain 4, [double crochet, chain 1] 11 times in ring. Join with slip stitch in 3rd chain of beginning chain. Fasten off—12 chain 1-spaces.

Round 2 With C, join with slip stitch in any chain 1-space, (chain 2, double crochet 2 together) in same space, [chain 2, cluster in next chain 1-space] 11 times, chain 2. Join with slip stitch in beginning 2-double crochet cluster. Fasten off—12 chain 2-spaces.

Round 3 With F, join with slip stitch in any chain 2-space, chain 1, single crochet in same space, [chain 5, single crochet in next chain 2-space] 11 times, chain 5. Join with slip stitch in first single crochet. Fasten off.

Round 4 With A, join with slip stitch in any chain 5-space, (chain 2, double crochet 2 together, chain 2, cluster) in same space, *chain 3, skip next chain 5-space, single crochet in next single crochet, chain 3, skip next chain 5-space, [cluster, chain 2, cluster, chain 4, cluster, chain 2, cluster] in next chain 5-space; repeat from * 3 more times, ending [cluster, chain 2, cluster] in beginning chain 5-space, chain 1, double crochet in top of beginning 2-double crochet cluster.

Round 5 Same as Square 1 round 4.

ASSEMBLY

Using large-eyed, blunt needle, weave in all ends except for long tail at end. Use tails to sew squares into a 5 x 7 array according to assembly diagram (page 37). To sew: Thread tail of one square on large-eyed, blunt needle. With wrong sides together and lining up stitches, hold together with next square and whipstitch through back loop only of 18 single crochet per side of each square. Sew 5 rows of 7 squares each in the same

manner. With wrong sides facing, align two 7-square strips and whip-stitch together through the back loops. Continue to sew remaining strips to first two.

EDGING

With right side facing, begin at any corner. Note: You may wish to mark the chain-space or stitch at each of the four corners of afghan for clarity; move markers up as you go. **Round 1 (RS)** With A, join with slip stitch through back loop only of middle (3rd) single crochet in corner, chain 1, single crochet through back loop in same single crochet, *single crochet through back loop in next 17 single crochet of same square, single crochet through back loop in each of next 18 single crochet on each square across length of side, except in last single crochet make a corner of [single crochet through back loop, chain 2, single crochet through back loop] rotate; repeat from * 3 more times, ending single crochet through back loop in same corner single crochet as beginning, chain 2. Join with slip stitch in first single crochet. Fasten off—432

single crochet + 4 corner chain 2-spaces.

Round 2 (RS) With B, join with slip stitch in beginning corner chain 2-space, chain 2, double crochet 2 together in same space, *[chain 1, skip next single crochet, cluster in next single crochet] across to next corner chain 2-space, chain 1, [cluster, chain 1, cluster] in corner chain 2-space; repeat from * 3 more times, ending with cluster in same corner chain 2-space as beginning, chain 1. Join with slip stitch in first 2-double crochet cluster. Fasten off.

Round 3 (RS) With C, join with slip stitch in beginning corner chain 1-space, chain 1, single crochet in same space, 2 single crochet in each chain 1-space across to next corner chain 1-space, [single crochet, chain 2, single crochet] in next corner chain-space; repeat from * 3 more times, ending with single crochet in same corner chain 1-space as beginning, chain 2. Join with slip stitch in first single crochet. Fasten off. Turn.

Round 4 (WS) With F, join with slip stitch in beginning corner chain 2-space, chain 3, 2 dc in same

space, skip next single crochet, *[single crochet in next single crochet, skip next single crochet, shell in next single crochet, skip next single crochet] across, single crochet in last single crochet before corner chain 2-space, 5 double crochet in corner chain-space, skip next single crochet; repeat from * 3 more times, ending 2 double crochet in same corner chain 2-space as beginning. Join with slip stitch in 3rd chain of beginning chain. Fasten off. Turn.

Round 5 (RS) With C, join with slip stitch in same corner double crochet, chain 3, 2 double crochet in same double crochet, single crochet in next double crochet, *[shell in next single crochet, single crochet in 2nd double crochet of next shell] across to next corner shell, placing single crochet in 2nd double crochet of corner shell, 5 double crochet in next double crochet, single crochet in next double crochet; repeat from * twice, ending at last corner shell, single crochet in 2nd double crochet of corner shell, 2 double crochet in same double crochet as beginning. Join with slip stitch in

3rd chain of beginning chain. Fasten off. Turn.

Round 6 (WS) With E, join with slip stitch in same corner double crochet, chain 3, double crochet in same double crochet, single crochet in next double crochet, *[shell in next single crochet, single crochet in 2nd double crochet of next shell] across to next corner shell, placing single crochet in 2nd double crochet of corner shell, shell in next double crochet, single crochet in next double crochet; repeat from * twice, ending with single crochet in 2nd double crochet of corner shell, double crochet in same double crochet as beginning. Join with slip stitch in 3rd chain of beginning chain. Fasten off. Turn.

Round 7 (RS) With C, join with slip stitch in same corner double crochet, chain 1, single crochet in same double crochet, single crochet in each double crochet and single crochet around, making a corner of [single crochet, chain 2, single crochet] in 2nd double crochet of each corner shell, end with single crochet in same double crochet as beginning, chain 2. Join with slip stitch in first single crochet. Fasten off.

Using large-eyed, blunt needle, weave in ends. Block afghan to 36" x 48" (91 x 122 cm).

ASSEMBLY DIAGRAM

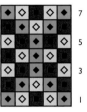

■ Square 1

◇ Square 2

■ Square 3

HOLIDAY ORNAMENTS AND GIFT TAGS

DESIGNED BY ANDI SMITH FOR KNITBRIT
KNIT/EASY

These quickie ornaments are great for decorating trees, tagging gifts, or just about anything else you can think of!

SIZE

Each ornament and gift tag is approximately 3–4" (7.5–10 cm)

MATERIALS

 LION BRAND® LION® WOOL
100% WOOL
3 OZ (85 G) 158 YD (144 M) BALL

1 ball #113 Scarlet

 LION BRAND® TIFFANY
100% NYLON
1¾ OZ (50 G) 137 YD (125 M) BALL

1 ball #100 White

- Size 8 (5 mm) needles
- Size G-6 (4 mm) crochet hook
- Large-eyed, blunt needle

GAUGE

Gauge is not critical.

NOTE

One ball of each will make at least one of each ornament type.

STITCH EXPLANATION

Raglan top shaping

Row 1 Knit 1, slip slip knit, knit to last 3 stitches, knit 2 stitches together, knit 1.

Row 2 Purl.

These two rows form the raglan shaping for the front, back, and sleeves.

SWEATER ORNAMENT

BACK

With knitting needles and yarn A, cast on 16 stitches and work 3 rows of knit 1, purl 1 rib, work 6 rows of stockinette stitch.
Work raglan shaping until 8 stitches rem. Bind off.

FRONT

Work as for back from * to *.
Work 2 rows of raglan shaping.
Divide for neck as follows:

Row 1 Knit 1, slip slip knit, knit 2, k2tog, turn—5 stitches.

Row 2 Purl.

Row 3 Knit 1, slip slip knit, knit 2 stitches together, turn—3 stitches.

Row 4 Purl.

Row 5 Bind off.

Work the opposite side of the sweater, reversing the shaping.

SLEEVES—MAKE 2

Cast on 12 stitches in A and work 3 rows of rib.
Beginning with a purl row, work 5 rows of stockinette stitch, then raglan shaping until 4 stitches remain. Bind off.

FINISHING

Sew the raglan sleeves to the back and front of the body, then sew side seams. Weave in loose ends.

Fluffy Collar

With G hook and 2 strands of B, single crochet in each stitch around neck hole for 2 rounds. Finish off and weave in ends.

Hanging Loop

With G hook and A, chain 25 and fasten off. Sew securely into the back of the sweater between the shoulders.

SANTA HAT ORNAMENT

Using knitting needles and A, cast on 28 stitches and work 4 rows of stockinette stitch. Place marker after the 14th stitch.

Row 5 Knit 1, slip slip knit, knit to 3 stitches before marker, knit 2 stitches together, knit 2, slip slip knit, knit to last 3 stitches, knit 2 stitches together, knit 1.

Row 6 Purl.

Row 7 Knit.

Row 8 Purl.

Repeat last 4 rows until 8 stitches remain. Work 2 rows in stockinette stitch, bind off.
Sew up the side seam and press lightly.

HAT BAND

Using 2 strands of B and G hook, single crochet in each stitch, working six rounds. Close and weave in ends.

Hat Bobble

Using 2 strands of B and G hook, single crochet in each stitch, close with a slip stitch—8 single crochet.

Round 2 Work 2 single crochet in each loop, close with a slip stitch—16 single crochet.

Round 3 Same as row 2 (32 single crochet), close with a slip stitch and cut yarn, leaving a 12" (30.5 cm) tail. Thread the yarn onto a large-eyed, blunt needle and work in and out of each single crochet with a running stitch. Pull tightly to form a ball and fasten off securely. Attach a hanging loop in the same way as for the sweater.

HANGING WREATH ORNAMENT

Using knitting needles and A, cast on 50 stitches.

Row 1 Purl.

Row 2 Knit.

Row 3 Knit.

Row 4 Purl.

Repeat rows 3 and 4 three more times.
Cut yarn, leaving a 12" (30.5 cm) tail, and thread through all stitches. Pull tightly to form a circle and sew up the side seam.
With G hook and 2 strands of yarn B, single crochet in each stitch around inside and outside edges, working in the round for three rounds. fasten off and weave in loose ends.
Attach a hanging loop in the same way as for the sweater.

3.
PET PROJECTS

Why should you have all the fun? Fido and
Fluffy like yarn, too—just ask any cat or dog
eyeing the skeins in your stash. Projects for
your pets are a great way to use up stash yarn
(and give you an excuse to buy new yarn)!

CAT SUSHI

DESIGN BY ANDI SMITH
CROCHET/EASY

Real sushi makes a mess on your carpet—crochet some for
your cat instead!

SIZE

One size approximately 4½"
long x 2½" wide (11 x 6 cm)

MATERIALS

 LION BRAND® LION® WOOL
100% WOOL

3 OZ (85 G) 158 YD (144 M) BALL

1 ball each #099 Winter White (A),
#123 Sage (B), and #133 Pumpkin
(C), or colors of your choice

- Size G-6 (4 mm) crochet hook
- Polyfill stuffing or batting
- Catnip (optional, but 9 out
  of 10 cats recommend)
- Large-eyed, blunt needle

GAUGE

Gauge is not critical. Your cat
won't mind if the toy is a little
over- or undersized!

RICE

With A, chain 27, turn.
Round 1 Half double crochet into
2nd loop from hook then each
loop, working through both loops,
turn—25 half double crochet.
Repeat round 1 until 16 rounds are
completed. Fasten off yarn.
Fold in half and sew 1½" (3.75 cm)
down each end of seam. Open
the rice out until the seam is
in the center, and sew down the
end seams.
Turn right side out and stuff firmly
with batting and catnip. Close
center seam.

SALMON

With C, chain 22, turn.
Round 1 Half double crochet into
2nd loop from hook then each
loop, working through both
loops—20 half double crochet.
Repeat round 1 five times.

Fasten off yarn and sew salmon
securely to top of rice.

NORI STRIP

Using B and large-eyed, blunt
needle, starting at the back of the
sushi, sew a chain stitch around
the center. Each stitch should be
about the length of a crochet chain.
Weave in ends.

CROCHET CAT BED

DESIGNED BY ANDI SMITH FOR KNITBRIT

CROCHET/BEGINNER

Cats love cozy little spaces—if you have a very small cat, you might want to make this bed slightly smaller.

SIZE

Sample shown Approximately 16" long x 12" wide (41 x 30.5 cm)

MATERIALS

 LION BRAND® BOLERO (A)
100% WOOL

3½ OZ (100 G) 55 YD (50 M) BALL

5 balls #206 Lime Blue, or color of your choice

 LION BRAND® TIFFANY (B)
100% NYLON

1¾ OZ (50 G) 137 YD (125 M) BALL

2 balls #105 Light Blue or color of your choice

- Size J-10 (6 mm) crochet hook
- Large-eyed, blunt needle

GAUGE

Gauge is not important for this pattern, but firm stitches are.

NOTES

Because of the width variances in Bolero, it may be necessary to add the occasional single crochet along the side edges. The single crochet stitches should run vertical to the previous row. If you find the stitches are leaning to the right, add an extra single crochet stitch.

BASE

Using 2 strands of A, chain 12. Work 2 single crochet into 3rd chain from hook, single crochet into each loop on chain, and 2 single crochet into last loop. Working in the round, continue to work single crochet into each loop and 2 single crochet on either side of the long ends, increasing a total of 4 single crochet each round until work measures 18" x 14" (45 x 35 cm).

SIDES

Row 1 Turn chain 1, single crochet into each loop on previous round. Join with slip stitch.
Rows 2–4 Chain 1, single crochet into each loop, join with a slip stitch.
Row 5 Chain 1, single crochet into front post of row 1 to form a band around sides. Join with slip stitch.
Rows 6–10 Work as Row 2.
Weave in all ends.

FUR TRIM

With 2 strands of B, chain 1, single crochet in each loop for 2 rounds, then fasten off.

SOPHIE DOG SWEATER

DESIGNED BY ANDI SMITH FOR KNITBRIT

KNIT/EASY

This is a no-cable, cabled-look sweater, suitable for confident beginners. A chain stitch detail is added after knitting to give the look of cables without the hassle of a cable needle.

SIZE

To fit a small dog
Neck 12" (30.5 cm)
Length 10" (25.4 cm)
Chest 16" (40.6 cm)

MATERIALS

 LION BRAND® WOOL-EASE® THICK & QUICK®
80% ACRYLIC, 20% WOOL
6 OZ (170 G) 106 YD (97 M) BALL

1 ball #189 Butterscotch, or color of your choice

• Size 9 (5.5 mm) needles
• Large-eyed, blunt needle

GAUGE

12 stitches = 4" (10 cm) in pattern

NOTE

This pattern is worked from the bottom up to the neck.

STITCH EXPLANATIONS

tw2 (Twist 2) Knit the second stitch on the left hand needle without taking it off the needle, knit the first stitch, then take both stitches off.

mb (Make Bobble) (Knit, purl, knit, purl, knit) into next stitch, turn, purl 5, turn, knit 3 together, knit 2 together, pass knit 3 together stitch over.

slip slip slip knit Slip 3 stitches, one at a time knitwise, then knit them all together.

STITCH PATTERN
(MULTIPLE OF 7 STITCHES)

Row 1 (Purl 1, tw2, purl 3, knit 1, purl 2), repeat to last 4 stitches, purl 1, tw2, purl 1.

Row 2 and every even row: Knit the knit stitches and purl the purl stitches.

Row 3 Purl 1, (tw2, purl 2, knit 3, purl 2), repeat to last 3 stitches, tw2, purl 1.

Row 5 Purl 1, (tw2, purl 1, knit 2, mb, knit 2, purl 1), repeat to last 3 stitches, tw2, purl 1.

Row 7 Repeat row 3.

Row 9 Repeat row 1.

Repeat rows 3–10.

BODY

Cast on 49 stitches and work 4 rows of knit 1, purl 1 rib and then work the stitch pattern until the body measures 6½" (16.3 cm), ending after working a wrong side row.

DIVIDE FOR LEGS

Row 1 With right side facing, and keeping the continuity of the pattern, work 8 stitches, place the next 5 stitches on a stitch holder, pattern 22 stitches, place 5 stitches on a stitch holder, work last 8 stitches in pattern.

Row 2 Pattern 8, cast on 5, pattern 22, cast on 5, pattern 8.

Row 3 (Knit, purl, knit, p2tog) repeat to last 3 stitches, knit, purl, knit—39 stitches.

Row 4 Work in knit 1, purl 1 rib.

Row 5 Rib 4 stitches, slip slip slip knit, (rib 7, slip slip slip knit) to last 2 stitches, rib 2—31 stitches.

Rows 6–16 Work in knit 1, purl 1 rib.

Bind off loosely.

LEGS

Work both legs the same.

Row 1 With right side of work facing, pick up the 5 stitches from holder then cast on 14 stitches—19 stitches.

Work 5 rows of knit 1, purl 1 rib and bind off loosely.

FINISHING

Using needle and length of yarn, chain stitch a diamond pattern along the edge of the diamond of knit stitches in each pattern. Each chain stitch should be the same size as a knitted stitch.

Turn the sweater inside out and sew the side seams of each leg and then attach the tube to the body evenly. Sew the body seam and weave in all ends.

HOLLY DOG SWEATER

DESIGNED BY ANDI SMITH FOR KNITBRIT

CROCHET/EASY

A Peter Pan collar and deep color give this canine couture that little something extra!

SIZE

To fit a small dog

Neck 14" (35.6 cm)

Length 8" (20.3 cm)

Chest 18" (45.7 cm)

MATERIALS

 LION BRAND® CHENILLE THICK & QUICK®

91% ACRYLIC 9% RAYON

100 YD (90 M) SKEIN (WEIGHT VARIES)

1 skein #106 Monarch, or color of your choice

- Size I-9 (5.5 mm) crochet hook
- Large-eyed, blunt needle

GAUGE

Gauge is not critical; however, if you'd like to size the sweater up or down slightly, try changing the hook size.

COLLAR

Chain 30, join with slip stitch.

Round 1 Chain 1, half double crochet into each loop, close with slip stitch—30 half double crochet.

Round 2 Chain 1, half double crochet into each loop, turn—30 half double crochet.

Round 3 Chain 1, half double crochet into each loop, turn—30 half double crochet.

Round 4 Chain 1, half double crochet into each loop, increasing 4 times evenly across round, turn—34 half double crochet.

Round 5 Chain 1, 3 half double crochet into first loop, half double crochet in each loop until last, 3 half double crochet into last loop, turn—40 half double crochet.

Round 6 Chain 1, single crochet all the way around the collar including up the V—approximately 47 single crochet.

Fasten off and break yarn.

BODY

Rejoin yarn on the bottom center of collar.

Round 1 Chain 1, half double crochet into each loop, close with a slip stitch—30 half double crochet.

Round 2 Chain 1, half double crochet into each loop, evenly increase 4 half double crochet across round, close with slip stitch—34 half double crochet.

Round 3 Chain 1, half double crochet into each loop, close with slip stitch—34 half double crochet.

Round 4 Chain 1, half double crochet into each loop, evenly increase 4 half double crochet across round, close with slip stitch—38 half double crochet.

Round 5 Chain 1, half double crochet into next 5 loops, chain 7, skip 7 on previous round and continue to half double crochet into each loop until 7 half double crochet away from end of round,

chain 7, close round with slip stitch.

Rounds 8–12 Chain 1, half double crochet into each loop, close with slip stitch—38 half double crochet.

Round 13 Chain 1, *decrease 1, half double crochet in next 3 loops; repeat from * to end—31 half double crochet.

Round 14 Single crochet into each loop, fasten off.

LEGS
Single crochet 16 times around leg hole for 2 rounds, fasten off. Repeat on other leg.

FINISHING
Weave in all ends.

DECORATIVE COLLAR

DESIGNED BY LISA WALKUP

KNIT/INTERMEDIATE

You know what they say about dogs looking like their owners. You can easily take this one step further by knitting a matching belt; simply add a few more inches to this pattern!

SIZE

Adjustable

Size shown 16" (40.5 cm) long

MATERIALS

 LION BRAND® LION® WOOL-EASE®

80% ACRYLIC, 20% WOOL

3 OZ (85 G) 197 YD (180 M) BALL

1 ball each #174 Avocado (MC) and 1 ball #195 Azalea Pink (CC), or colors of your choice

- 1 set of four size 2 (2.75 mm) double pointed needles, *or size to obtain gauge*
- 1 stitch marker
- Large-eyed, blunt needle
- 1 set of two metal 1 D-rings (available at fabric stores)

GAUGE

32 stitches and 26 rounds = 4" (10 cm) in stockinette stitch in the round. Note: The gauge is tighter than you would normally knit with a worsted weight yarn to create a stronger fabric.

Be sure to check your gauge.

NOTE

Make the collar at least 5" (12.5 cm) longer than the neck of your dog to allow for fastening.

COLLAR

With the main color, cast on 16 stitches. Arrange the stitches onto 3 double-pointed needles. Swap the first and last stitch to join your work by sliding the first stitch onto the third needle, and then passing the last stitch over the first stitch and sliding it onto the first needle. Be sure not to twist your stitches before making the join.

Knit 1 round with the main color. Place a stitch marker before the last stitch in your round to keep track of the end of the round. Slide the marker each time you get to it, knit the last stitch, and begin the new round.

Join the contrasting color and begin following the chart to work the 4 rounds of the houndstooth pattern. Carry along the unused color at the back, and switch when necessary. Be sure to keep the tension on the yarn snug, but not too tight.

Continue working in the hound-stooth pattern until the collar

measures the desired size.
Knit the last round using contrasting color.
Bind off.

FINISHING

Weave all ends into the inside of the tube. Sew the beginning and end of the tube closed. To hide the yarn ends inside the tube, cut the yarn close to the tube and push the end inside using the top of the yarn needle.

Flatten the tube, and thread one end through the 2 D-rings. Fold over 1" (2.5 cm) and sew down firmly to enclose the D-rings.

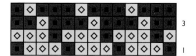

3

1

■ contrast color

◇ main color

4.
ADORN ME

Jewelry doesn't have to be metal! Try these
unique knit and crochet adornments and you'll
soon be covered in glitz. Remember, all that
glitters is not gold—sometimes, it's gold lamé!
Have fun and experiment with these projects.
After all, they don't eat up a lot of yarn because
they're so small.

SOLAR SYSTEM NECKLACE

DESIGNED BY VLADLENA BELOZEROVA

CROCHET/EASY

These necklaces are infinitely customizable, whether you want a single globe or a dozen baby planets orbiting your neck.

SIZE

One size fits most

MATERIALS

 LION BRAND® GLITTERSPUN
60% ACRYLIC, 27% CUPRO, 13% POLYESTER

1¾ OZ (50 G) 115 YD (105 M) BALL

1 ball #150 Silver, or color of your choice

- Size 7 (4.5 mm) steel crochet hook, or smallest hook size you can use to crochet with Glitterspun comfortably
- Necklace memory wire
- Clear thread or fishing line
- Stuffing material, such as polyfill or yarn scraps
- Medium-eyed, blunt needle
- Sewing needle
- Stitch marker

GAUGE

Checking gauge is not as critical as ensuring stitches are fairly tight. Use the smallest hook possible to work with the yarn.

NOTES

Rounds are worked in a spiral. Place a marker in the first stitch of the second round to mark the beginning of the round. Remove the marker when working the first stitch of each round, and replace it immediately into the stitch you just made.

LARGE BEAD

Chain 2.

Round 1 Work 6 single crochet in second chain from hook. Do not join; continue to work in a spiral— 6 single crochet.

Round 2 2 single crochet in each stitch around—12 single crochet.

Round 3 *Single crochet in next stitch, 2 single crochet in next stitch; repeat from * around—18 single crochet.

Round 4 *Single crochet in each of next 2 stitches, 2 single crochet in next stitch; repeat from * around— 24 single crochet.

Round 5 *Single crochet in each of next 3 stitches, 2 single crochet in next stitch; repeat from * around— 30 single crochet.

Round 6 Single crochet in each stitch around—30 single crochet.

Round 7 *Single crochet in each of next 4 stitches, skip next stitch; repeat from * around—24 single crochet.

Round 8 *Single crochet in each of next 3 stitches, skip next stitch; repeat from * around—18 single crochet.

Begin stuffing the bead with stuffing material as you work the following rounds.

Round 9 *Single crochet in each of next 2 stitches, skip next stitch; repeat from * around—12 single crochet.

Round 10 *Skip next stitch, single crochet in next stitch; repeat from * around. Join with slip stitch in first single crochet—6 single crochet. Fasten off.

With yarn needle, weave in ends.

SMALL BEAD

Chain 2.

Round 1 Work 6 single crochet in second stitch from hook. Do not join; continue to work in a spiral—6 single crochet.

Round 2 2 single crochet in each stitch around—12 single crochet.

Round 3 *Single crochet in next stitch, 2 single crochet in next stitch; repeat from * around—18 single crochet.

Round 4 *Single crochet in each of next 2 stitches, 2 single crochet in next stitch; repeat from * around—24 single crochet.

Round 5 Single crochet in each stitch around—24 single crochet.

Round 6 *Single crochet in each of next 3 stitches, skip next stitch; repeat from * around—18 single crochet.

Begin stuffing bead with stuffing material as you work the following rounds.

Round 7 *Single crochet in each of next 2 stitches, skip next stitch; repeat from * around—12 single crochet.

Round 8 *Skip next stitch, single crochet in next stitch; repeat from * around. Join with slip stitch in first single crochet—6 single crochet. Fasten off.

With yarn needle, weave in ends.

FINISHING

Measure the desired length around your neck and cut memory wire to length. Using invisible thread or clear fishing line, sew beads together and thread memory wire through the stuffed beads. You may also crochet a Glitterspun chain if you prefer.

SPARKLY ANKLE BRACELETS

DESIGNED BY MICHELE RITAN

CROCHET/INTERMEDIATE

You cannot have too many of these anklets! It's just not possible. They also look gorgeous on your wrists or even (if made longer) as necklaces.

SIZE

S (L)

Length Approximately 9.5 (12)" [23.75 (30) cm]

MATERIALS

 LION BRAND® LAMÉ

35% METALLIZED POLYESTER, 65% RAYON

⅔ OZ (19 G) 75 YD (67 M) SPOOL

1 spool #170 Goldenrod, or color of your choice

- Size C-2 (2.75 mm) crochet hook, *or size to obtain gauge*
- Size 6/0 glass or metal beads (also known as E beads): 24 (29); available at craft stores
- Dental floss threader for threading beads on yarn (optional)
- Clasp (lobster claw or barrel works well); available at craft stores
- Tapestry needle, size 18
- Fray Check

GAUGE

12 chains = 2" (5 cm).

Be sure to check your gauge.

BEADING NOTE

To thread the beads on the yarn, you can either use a dental floss threader or apply a bit of clear nail polish to firm it up.

YARN NOTE

Due to the metallic content, Lion Brand Lamé is a bit stiff. It will also curl up as you work. With a little practice, you may find it easy to work with. It much easier to use than wire, and creates a sparkly jewelry effect. It is not fragile. Don't be afraid to stretch it out as you go, and crochet firmly!

ANKLE BRACELET

Thread 24 (29) beads on the yarn using threading method of your choice. Slide them down so they are out the way for now, leaving a 15" (37.5 cm) tail.

Chain 50 (60) loosely. The chain stitches should be about ⅛–¼" (1 cm or less) in size. Chaining loosely will make the first row easy to do.

Chain 2 stitches tightly.

In the third chain from the hook (the first looser one), make one single crochet through the front loop of the chain. Continue with one single crochet through the front loop to the end of the row. Work with medium firmness for this row.

Chain 2. Turn.

The work will coil up after you complete the first row. Stretch the work to unkink it a bit. Or you can use an iron on the wool setting to stretch and flatten it out.

*Single crochet in each of next 2 stitches, through the front loop. Chain 3 firmly. Bring a bead up

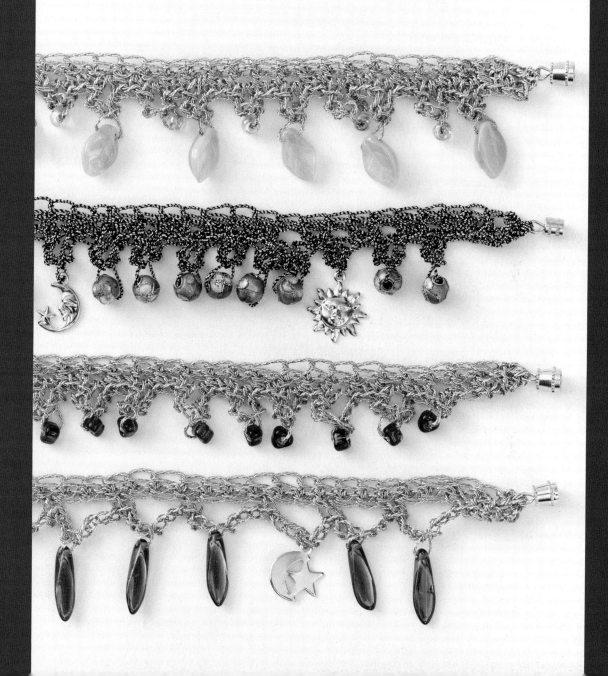

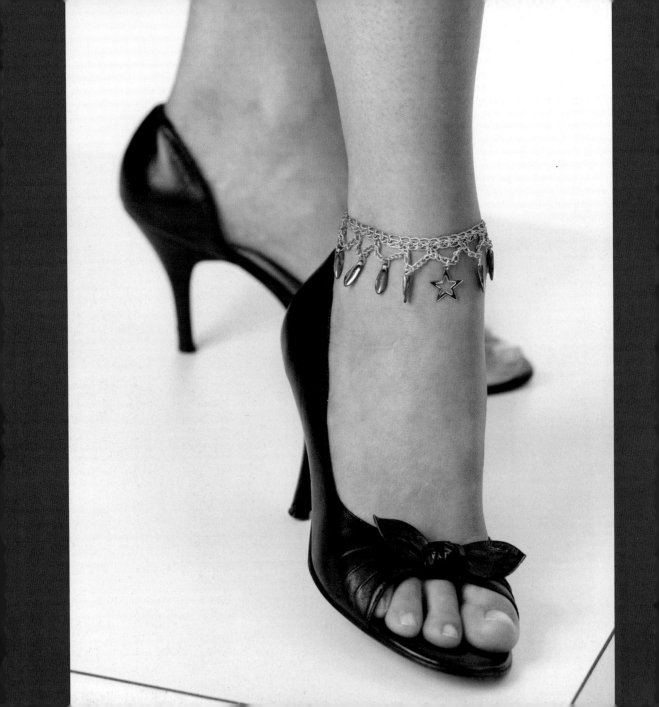

close to the stitch, then chain 1 to lock it securely in place.

Chain two more stitches firmly. Return to the base of the chain 3. Make one single crochet in this space.*

Repeat from * to * to end of row. Fasten off, leaving 15" (37.5 cm) tail.

FINISHING

Ironing your ankle bracelet is a very important final step. Yes, you can iron this fiber, up to 160 degrees. The wool setting on most irons is a good choice. Pull the beads downward gently to stretch the chained sections apart. Be careful not to burn your fingers! Block it to the shape you want and leave it to cool on the ironing board.

Thread one end of yarn through the tapestry needle. Thread through the metal loop on the end of the clasp. Sew securely to the end of the bracelet. Weave in ends. Repeat on the other end of the bracelet.

Use a drop of Fray Check to secure the ends.

Let your ankles sparkle!

VARIATIONS

This pattern lends itself to improvisation! Add or subtract stitches and beads to change the size. You could even make a necklace! Here are a couple of variations to start you thinking about the possibilities.

CLUSTER VARIATION

Use main pattern, but use clusters of three beads together rather than single beads. Just multiply the bead count by three and thread them on the yarn before you begin, as above.

DAGGER BEAD ANKLE BRACELET

This version substitutes size 19 (15 mm) dagger beads for 6/0 beads and measures approximately 12" (30.5 cm).

Follow main pattern until you complete the first row of single crochet, turn.

Stretch the work to unkink it a bit. Or you can use an iron on the wool setting to stretch and flatten it out.

Single crochet in each of next 2 stitches, through the top loop.

*Chain 3 firmly. Bring a dagger bead up close to the stitch, then

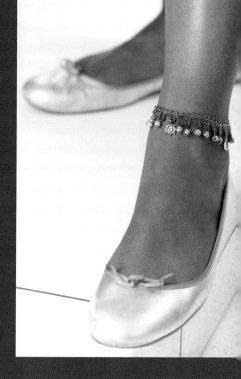

chain 1 to lock it securely in place.

Chain three more stitches firmly. Skip two single crochet. In the third single crochet, make one single crochet (this gives you a larger space between beads than the first pattern)*.

Repeat from * to * to end of row. Fasten off, leaving 15" (37.5 cm) tail. Finish as above.

5.
FELTED FUN

Felting is hot (water . . . with a cold rinse after-
ward)! You won't believe how quick and easy
these one-of-a-kind felted projects can be.

FELTING TECHNIQUE

When knitting or crocheting something you want to felt, you should use a larger needle or hook than you normally would. Swatching is of the utmost importance. Make a large swatch (at least an 8" [20.5 cm] square) and felt it exactly as you plan to felt your finished project. If you plan on doing any kind of "knit in" or yarn finishes, include a sample in your swatch.

There are three factors necessary for successful felting: water, temperature change, and agitation. Felting can be done by hand, in a bucket or the kitchen sink and using plenty of elbow grease, but it is much faster and easier to use a washing machine. Use a long wash setting with hot water and a cold rinse. Using your regular detergent or dish soap, add several sturdy items of clothing such as jeans, clean canvas shoes, or tennis balls. Towels will embed lint into the felt, so don't use them.

Regardless of the yarn you use, you may have to wash your project several times to felt it to your satisfaction. Felting is not an exact science. The water temperature, whether you have hard or soft water, the detergent, and the amount of agitation will all make a difference. The size of your project will also play a role. Large pieces felt differently than small pieces. To felt additionally, dry by machine on the regular setting until almost dry.

You can help your piece to fit the shape you want by manipulating it between cycles. Steam lightly to the desired shape. The piece will still be quite pliable before the final cold rinse. Your final project should have stitches that are hard to distinguish.

Felting can be used for trims and handles too. If you plan to make felted trim, make a few handles, fringes, and webbing strips at the same time and wash them all together.

Before felting

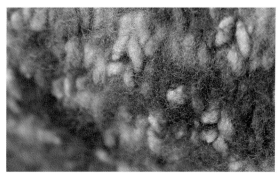

After felting

GREEK KEY COFFEE COZIES

DESIGNED BY SHARLEEN MORCO

KNIT/EASY

Inspired by the Greek diner coffee cups ubiquitous on the streets of New York City, these coffee cup cozies can be made two ways—knit, or knit then felted—in two sizes. Try them all! We are happy to serve them to you.

SIZE

S (M/L)

Circumference before felting

Approximately 9" (10½)" [22.5 (26.5 cm)]

Height before felting

Approximately 4½"

Circumference after felting

Approximately 8 (9)" [20 (22.5) cm]

Height after felting

Approximately 3" (7.5 cm)

MATERIALS

 LION BRAND® LION® WOOL

100% WOOL

3 OZ (85 G) 158 YD (144 M) BALL

1 ball each #099 Winter White (A) and #110 Cadet Blue (B), or colors of your choice

- 1 set size 8 (5 mm) straight needles, *or size to obtain gauge*
- Large-eyed, blunt needle

GAUGE

8 stitches + 10 rows = 2" (5 cm) in stockinette stitch.

Be sure to check your gauge.

COFFEE CUP COZY

For small size:

With A, cast on 36 stitches.

Row 1 Knit.

Row 2 Purl.

Row 3 With B, knit.

Rows 4–5 With A, work 2 rows in stockinette stitch.

Row 6 With B, purl.

Rows 7–8 With A, work 2 rows in stockinette stitch.

Rows 9–13 Work rows 1–5 of Greek Key Chart.

Rows 14–15 With A, work 2 rows in stockinette stitch.

Row 16 With B, purl.

Rows 17–18 With A, work 2 rows in stockinette stitch.

Row 19 With B, knit.

Rows 20–21 With A, work 2 rows in stockinette stitch.

Row 22 With B, purl.

Row 23 With A, knit.

Rows 24 With B, purl.

Rows 25 With A, knit.

Bind off.

For medium/large size:

With A, cast on 42 stitches.

Row 1 Knit.

Row 2 Purl.

Row 3 With B, knit.

Rows 4–5 With A, work 2 rows in stockinette stitch.

Row 6 With B, purl.

Rows 7–8 With A, work 2 rows in stockinette stitch.

Rows 9–13 Work rows 1–5 of Greek Key Chart, repeating chart around cozy.

Rows 14–15 With A, work two rows in stockinette stitch.

Row 16 With B, purl.

Rows 17–18 With A, work 2 rows in stockinette stitch.

Row 19 With B, knit.

Rows 20–21 With A, work 2 rows in stockinette stitch.

Row 22 With B, purl.

Row 23 With A, knit.

Row 24 With B, purl.

Row 25 With A, knit.

Bind off.

FINISHING

Secure or weave in the ends. Using hot water and a little bit of mild soap, hand-felt the coffee cozy by rubbing it with your hands and fingers. Continue until it measures roughly 3" (7.5 cm) in height and has an 8" (20 cm) circumference.

GREEK KEY CHART

◆ contrast color

· main color

AIRLINE PILLOW

DESIGNED BY CHRISTINE L. WALTER

KNIT/INTERMEDIATE

Sometimes flying can be stressful—why not turn it into a luxurious spa-nap? With this cashmere neck pillow, you can (even if you're still on the ground)!

SIZE

Before felting
Approximately 14" x 17" (35.5 x 43 cm)
After felting and stuffing
Approximately 13" x 16" (33 x 40.5 cm)

MATERIALS

LION BRAND® LION® CASHMERE BLEND
72% MERINO WOOL, 14% NYLON, 14% CASHMERE
1½ OZ (40 G) 84 YD (71 M) BALL

4 balls #153 Black (A), or color of your choice

LION BRAND® TIFFANY
100% NYLON
1¾ OZ (50 G) 137 YD (125 M) BALL

1 ball #153 Black (B), or color of your choice

- Size 10½ (6.5 mm) double-pointed knitting needles, *or size to obtain gauge*
- Stitch marker
- Large-eyed, blunt needle
- Polyfill or buckwheat hulls, for stuffing

GAUGE

Before felting: 16 stitches and 23 rows = 4" (10 cm) in stockinette stitch.
After felting: 16 stitches and 23 rows = approx. 3.5 (9 cm) by 3¼ (8.25 cm) in stockinette stitch.
Be sure to check your gauge.

NOTE

The pillow is worked in the round using short-row shaping to create the U shape.

PILLOW

Using double-pointed needle and one strand each of A and B held together, cast on 40 stitches. Join, being careful not to twist the stitches, and knit 1 row. Place marker for beginning of round. Do not turn but continue working in the round as follows.

FUR TRIM

*Round 1 Purl.
Round 2 Knit.*
Repeat these two rows twice more. Break B.

BODY

With A, work 36 rows of stockinette. **Turn corner using short rows:
Row 1 Knit to last 2 stitches, wrap and turn.
Row 2 Purl to last 2 stitches, wrap and turn.

Row 3 Knit to last 3 stitches, wrap and turn.
Row 4 Purl to last 3 stitches, wrap and turn.
Continue working short rows as established until center 4 stitches remain and 17 stitches are wrapped on either side of center stitches. Next, work completion rows as follows:
Row 1 With RS facing, knit to first wrapped stitch, knit stitch with the wrap, wrap and turn.
Row 2 With WS facing, purl to first wrapped stitch, purl stitch with the wrap, wrap and turn.
Repeat these 2 rows until all wrapped stitches have been worked.**
Resume working in rounds and work 28 rows in stockinette stitch, then repeat from ** to ** for next corner. Work an additional 36 rows

in stockinette stitch. Repeat fur trim for second edge as follows: Join B, knit 1 round with both A and B, then repeat the fur trim rounds from * to *. Cast off and break yarns. Weave in ends and close up any gaps before felting.

FINISHING

Felt pillow either by hand or machine, following directions on page 71, until no stitch definition remains. Block pillow lightly by laying it flat and allowing it to dry in place. If desired and to reduce the fuzziness of the fabric, lightly shave using a disposable razor. Fill pillow with polyester stuffing or buckwheat. Sew ends closed.

FELTED NEWSBOY HAT

DESIGNED BY LAURA KILLORAN FOR CROSHAY DESIGN
CROCHET/EASY

Extra! Extra! This jaunty hat will make you the talk of the town.

SIZE

Circumference before felting
27" (68.5 cm)
Circumference after felting
23" (58.5 cm)

MATERIALS

 LION BRAND® LION® WOOL
100% WOOL
3 OZ (85 G) 158 YD (144 M) BALL

2 balls #147 Purple (A) and
1 ball #149 Pearl Gray (B), or
colors of your choice

• Size M/N-13 (9 mm) crochet
  hook, *or size to obtain gauge*
• Large-eyed, blunt needle

GAUGE

Before felting 11 single crochet and
13 rows = 4" (10 cm).
Be sure to check your gauge.

NOTES

Crown is worked in joined rounds;
do not turn work after each round.
The first stitch of each round is
worked in the same stitch as the
one you joined to end the last
round.

HAT

With A, chain 4. Join with slip
stitch to form ring.
Round 1 Chain 1, 8 single crochet
into ring. Join with slip stitch in
first single crochet—8 single
crochet.
Round 2 Chain 1, 2 single crochet
in each single crochet around. Join
with slip stitch in first single
crochet—16 single crochet.
Round 3 Chain 1, single crochet in
first single crochet, 2 single crochet
in next single crochet, *single
crochet in next single crochet, 2
single crochet in next single
crochet; repeat from * around. Join
with slip stitch in first single
crochet—24 single crochet.
Round 4 Chain 1, single crochet in
each of first 2 single crochet, 2
single crochet in next single
crochet, *single crochet in each
of next 2 single crochet, 2 single
crochet in next single crochet;
repeat from * around. Join with slip
stitch in first single crochet—32
single crochet.
Round 5 Chain 1, single crochet in
first single crochet, single crochet
in each of next 2 single crochet, 2
single crochet in next single
crochet, *single crochet in each
of next 3 single crochet, 2 single
crochet in next single crochet;
repeat from * around. Join with slip
stitch in first single crochet—40
single crochet.
Round 6 Chain 1, single crochet in
first single crochet, single crochet
in each single crochet around. Join
with slip stitch in first single
crochet.
Round 7 Chain 1, single crochet in
first single crochet, single crochet
in each of next 3 single crochet, 2

single crochet in next single crochet, *single crochet in each of next 4 single crochet, 2 single crochet in next single crochet; repeat from * around. Join with slip stitch in first single crochet—48 single crochet.

Round 8 Repeat round 6.

Round 9 Chain 1, single crochet in first single crochet, single crochet in each of next 4 single crochet, 2 single crochet in next single crochet, *single crochet in each of next 5 single crochet, 2 single crochet in next single crochet; repeat from * around. Join with slip stitch in first single crochet—56 single crochet.

Round 10 Repeat Round 6.

Round 11 Chain 1, single crochet in first single crochet, single crochet in each of next 5 single crochet, 2 single crochet in next single

crochet, *single crochet in each of next 6 single crochet, 2 single crochet in next single crochet; repeat from * around. Join with slip stitch in first single crochet—64 single crochet.

Round 12 Repeat round 6.

Round 13 Chain 1, single crochet in first single crochet, single crochet in each of next 6 single crochet, 2 single crochet in next single crochet, *single crochet in each of next 7 single crochet, 2 single crochet in next single crochet; repeat from * around. Join with slip stitch in first single crochet—72 single crochet.

Round 14 Repeat round 6.

Round 15 Chain 1, single crochet in first single crochet, single crochet in each of next 7 single crochet, *2 single crochet in next single crochet, single crochet in each of next 17 single crochet; repeat from * 3 times, 2 single crochet in next single crochet, single crochet in each of last 9 single crochet. Join with slip stitch in first single crochet—76 single crochet.

Round 16 Repeat round 6.

Round 17 Chain 1, single crochet in first single crochet, single crochet in each of next 8 single crochet, *2

single crochet in next single crochet, single crochet in each of next 18 single crochet; repeat from * 3 times, 2 single crochet in next single crochet, single crochet in each of last 9 single crochet. Join with slip stitch in first single crochet—80 single crochet.

Rounds 18–21 Repeat round 6.

Round 22 Drop A to the back, join B, chain 1, single crochet in first single crochet, single crochet in each single crochet around. Join with slip stitch in first single crochet.

Round 23 Drop B, pick up A, chain 1, single crochet through back loop only in first single crochet, single crochet through back loop only in each single crochet around. Join with slip stitch in first single crochet through back loop only.

Rounds 24–26 Chain 1, single crochet in first single crochet, single crochet in each single crochet around. Join with slip stitch in first single crochet.

Round 27 With B, repeat round 22.

Round 28 With A, repeat round 23.

Round 29 Chain 1, single crochet in first single crochet and in each single crochet around. Join with slip stitch in first single crochet.

Round 30 Chain 1, single crochet in each of next 3 single crochet, single crochet 2 together over next 2 single crochet, *single crochet in each of next 7 single crochet, single crochet 2 together over next 2 single crochet; repeat from * around, ending single crochet in each of last 3 single crochet. Join with slip stitch in first single crochet—71 single crochet.

Round 31 With B, repeat round 22.

Round 32 With A, repeat round 23.

Round 33 Chain 1, skip first single crochet, single crochet in each of next 2 single crochet, *single crochet 2 together over next 2 single crochet, single crochet in each of next 2 single crochet; repeat from * around. Join with slip stitch in first single crochet—53 single crochet.

Round 34 With B, repeat round 22.

Round 35 With A, repeat round 23. Drop hook from loop, but do not fasten off yarn. The end of round 35 is the center back.

BRIM

Note: Work back and forth, turning after each row.

With right side facing, count 17 stitches from center back, and join A with slip stitch.

Row 1 Chain 1, single crochet in same stitch as join, single crochet in each of next 18 single crochet. Turn—19 single crochet.

Row 2 Chain 1, skip first single crochet, *single crochet in each of next 3 single crochet, 2 single crochet in next single crochet; repeat from * once, single crochet in next single crochet, **2 single crochet in next single crochet, single crochet in each of next 3 single crochet; repeat from ** once. Turn—21 single crochet.

Row 3 Chain 1, skip first single crochet, single crochet in each of next 19 single crochet. Turn—19 single crochet.

Row 4 Repeat row 2.

Row 5 Repeat row 3.

Row 6 Chain 1, skip first single crochet, *single crochet in each of next 5 single crochet, 2 single crochet in next single crochet; repeat from * once, single crochet in each of next 5 single crochet. Turn—19 single crochet.

Row 7 Chain 1, skip first single

crochet, single crochet in each of next 17 single crochet. Fasten off. Resume with A at center back.

Round 36 Chain 1, single crochet in first single crochet, single crochet in each single crochet around, working 9 stitches on each side of brim and 17 stitches across the front of brim. Fasten off A.

Round 37 With B, chain 1, single crochet in first single crochet, single crochet in each single crochet around. Fasten off.

FINISHING

With large-eyed, blunt needle, weave in ends.

Felt until finished hat measures 23" (58.5 cm) around, or to desired fit. You may felt by hand in the sink (be sure to wear gloves!) or in the washing machine with a hot cycle/cold rinse. Keep an eye on the hat as it is agitating in the washer—some machines work faster than others, and if you don't check it every few minutes, you may end up with a hat sized for Scott the Bear (page 15)!

6.
BAG OF TRICKS

Sometimes gifts need extra-special packaging, and these bags fit the bill. Of course, many of the purses featured in this chapter are exceptional gifts themselves. If you plan on making several bags for different friends, just choose a variety of colorways and color combinations to make each bag unique.

PERSONALIZING YOUR BAGS

LININGS

A well-built lining will make your bag durable and sturdy while protecting the yarn and seams from snagging or wearing on the inside. Lining a bag offers an interesting alternative to knit or crocheted patterns that aren't reversible, and at the same time enhances the overall design of your bag. Linings can be machine- or hand-stitched, half-lined or fully lined; they can even be constructed without any sewing.

Linings can maintain the shape of your bag and provide stability, especially when working with soft or stretchy yarns. Without the lining, some bags would collapse under the weight of the yarn. The linings also act as a barrier to prevent the yarn from catching on the inside. Commercial felt (or ultrasuede) won't fray, so there is no need to finish the seams.

INTERFACING

Interfacing your bag is a practical choice and there are many fun and creative ways to do it. Most reinforcement materials were designed for other crafts (needlepoint) or purposes (gardening).

One of the most practical products on the market is plastic canvas mesh. It is a plastic mesh sold in 13.5" by 11" (34.5 x 28 cm) sheets, 4" (10 cm) circles, as well as all kinds of novelty shapes (stars and hearts). It is manufactured in several gauges to match different weight yarns. Plastic canvas was originally designed for three-dimensional needlepoint and is sold in many different colors. The plastic is sturdy and the holes in the grid make it easy to sew. It can also be used more traditionally and wrapped (or covered) in the same yarn.

GREAT HARDWARE

The right hardware can change the look of a basic knit or crochet bag into a finished, sophisticated design. If you want to contrast or complement the knit or crochet body of your bag with purchased hardware, there are many options. Handles come in hundreds of styles and all kinds of materials. Web sites like mjtrim.com and umx.info/purse-handbag-cat1.htm sell handbag handles made from a variety of materials and in a vast range of styles, shapes, and sizes. Handles can also be purchased from craft stores, such as Michael's and JoAnn's. For a unique, vintage look, buy bags at thrift shops and reuse the handles and other hardware.

Other purse-making supplies such as buckles, D-rings, magnet snap closures, swivel clasps, and tab closures are fun to experiment with.

FUN FINISHES

Even the simplest bag becomes a stunning success when you use a great finishing technique. Finish your bag with a reinforcing stitching technique or jazz up your bag with self trims like pom-poms, tassels, rope cords, and webbing.

STITCHES

These stitches can be done in the same yarn as your project or in a contrasting yarn or thread. When using any of these stitches on a purchased fabric such as felt or ultrasuede use a cotton embroidery floss instead of yarn.

Running Stitch (used to top stitch)

This basic sewing stitch looks fresh and new when done with yarn on knitted or crocheted fabric. Use a running stitch to topstitch webbing, handles, and bag closures. Use a blunt, large-eyed needle and insert it into the fabric from the wrong side to the right side, leaving a 3" (7.5 cm) tail of yarn to weave in later. Insert the needle back to the wrong side and be careful not to pull the yarn too tightly or it will distort the fabric. Continue for desired length and fasten off on wrong side of piece.

Blanket Stitch

Sometimes called buttonhole stitch, blanket stitch is a great finishing touch on edges. Blanket stitch can be used to finish handles and bag edges or to embellish.

Step 1. Using a blunt, large-eyed yarn needle, secure the yarn by gently attaching it to a stitch on the wrong side of work. Leave a 3" (8 cm) tail to weave in later.

Step 2. Draw the needle through to the right side of work, close to the edge.

Step 3. Bring the needle above the yarn and insert it a couple of stitches to the right of where you first inserted it (see illustration A).

Step 4. Pull the needle past the edge of the bag to complete the stitch.

Repeat steps 3 and 4, inserting the needle the same number of stitches apart for even spacing.

Invisible Seaming

Invisible seaming is a sturdy, invisible way to sew two panels together. It can be sewn (vertically) on the side seam or (horizontally) on two bound-off edges.

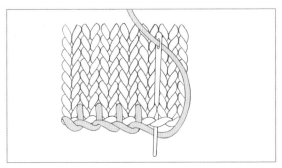

A. Blanket stitch.

B. Invisible seam—stockinette stitch.

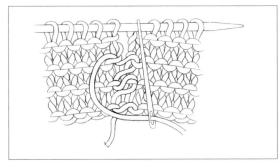

C. Invisible seam—garter stitch.

Invisible seaming is worked on the right side, with a long yarn end (add a length from the initial cast-on or bound-off edge) and a blunt, large-eyed sewing needle. Start at the upper or lower edge by joining the two edges. Begin the seaming by catching two horizontal bars just inside the edge of the first stitch and carry the thread across to the other side, stitching under the next pair of bars inside the edge of the first stitch (see illustrations B and C). Pull the sewing thread every couple of stitches but do not gather. There should be some ease. The seam will join together and be nearly invisible. The same technique can be used to join two bound-off edges.

ROPE CORDS

Cut six strands of yarn, each approximately 94" (239 cm) long. (If you are using a bulky yarn for the tie, you may want to use fewer than six strands of yarn to make the cord.) Hold the lengths together and tie a knot at each end. Anchor one end and twist the other end clockwise many times until the piece is very tight and almost kinked. Hold the rope in the center and release both ends, allowing them to wrap around each other.

CROCHET FLOWERS

Chain 4. Join with slip stitch to form a ring.

Round 1 Chain 1 (counts as 1 single crochet), work 11 single crochet into ring. Join round with slip stitch in chain-1.

Round 2 (Chain 3, skip next stitch, single crochet in next stitch) 6 times—6 chain-3 loops.

Round 3 (In next chain-3 loop work [single crochet, half double crochet, 3 double crochet, half double crochet, single crochet]) 6 times. Join round with a slip stitch in first single crochet. Fasten off.

KNIT FLOWERS

Cast on 42 stitches.

Row 1 (wrong side) Purl.

Row 2 Knit 2, *knit 1, slip this stitch back to left needle, lift next 5 stitches on left needle over this stitch and off needle, yarn over twice, knit the first stitch again, knit 2; repeat from *—27 stitches.

Row 3 Purl 1, *purl 2 together, drop 1 of the yarn over loops, (knit into the front and back) twice in remaining yarn over of previous row, purl 1; repeat from * to last stitch, purl 1—32 stitches.

Row 4 Knit 1, *knit 3 together; repeat from *, end knit 1—12 stitches.

Row 5 *Purl 2 together; repeat from *—6 stitches; slip 2nd, 3rd, 4th, 5th, and 6th stitches over first stitch. Fasten off and sew seam.

Make another if desired. Use contrasting color to attach to bag.

GLITTERSPUN GIFT BAG

DESIGNED BY CHRISSY GARDINER

KNIT/BEGINNER

Sometimes even presents need their own knits! Wrap them in one of these reusable gift bags and watch the recipient's eyes light up.

SIZE

6" wide x 9.5" high (15 x 24 cm)

MATERIALS

 LION BRAND® GLITTERSPUN
60% ACRYLIC, 27% CUPRO, 13% POLYESTER

1¾ OZ (50 G) 115 YD (105 M) BALL

1 ball #135 Bronze, or color of your choice

- Size 7 (4.5 mm) straight needles
- Large-eyed, blunt needle
- Fray Check or sewing needle and matching thread for finishing drawstring ends (available in craft and sewing stores)

GAUGE

18 stitches and 32 rows = 4" (10 cm) in stockinette stitch.
Gauge is not critical for this project.

GIFT BAG

Cast on 30 stitches. Starting with a knit row, work 1" (2.5 cm) in stockinette stitch. End with a purl row.
Eyelet Row (RS) Knit 2, *knit 2 stitches together, yarn over; repeat from * to last stitch, knit 2.
Work in stockinette stitch until piece measures 19" (48 cm) from beginning, ending with a purl row.
Eyelet Row (RS) Knit 2, *knit 2 stitches together, yarn over; repeat from * to last stitch, knit 2.
Work in stockinette stitch for 1" more (2.5 cm).
Bind off.

FINISHING

Fold bag in half with eyelet rows together and seam sides. Weave in all ends and block lightly.

DRAWSTRINGS—MAKE 2

Cut a piece of yarn 54" (135 cm) long. Tie one end to a doorknob and the other to a pencil or double-pointed needle. Twist the needle clockwise until the yarn is tightly twisted. Keeping the yarn taut, fold it in half. Remove the yarn from the doorknob and pencil and let it twist onto itself. Tie a knot about 1" (2.5 cm) from each end. Treat cut ends with Fray Check or whip stitch with sewing needle and thread.
Thread one drawstring through the eyelet row of each side of bag.

STARFLOWER SATCHEL

DESIGNED BY KATHRYN BECKERDITE

KNIT/EASY

This charming small handbag can be worked in two colors, as shown, or in one. Its star shape provides plenty of visual interest.

SIZE

Height 6" (15 cm)
Diameter 7" (17.5 cm)

MATERIALS

 LION BRAND® WOOL-EASE®
THICK & QUICK®
80% ACRYLIC/20% WOOL
6 OZ (170 G) 108 YD (98 M) BALL

1 ball each #106 Sky Blue (A) and #133 Pumpkin (B), or colors of your choice

• size 13 (9 mm) double-pointed needles
• 16" size 13 (9 mm) circular needle
• Stitch marker
• Stitch holders or waste yarn
• Large-eyed, blunt needle

GAUGE

12 stitches and 16 rows = 4" (10 cm) in stockinette stitch.
Gauge is not critical for this project.

STITCH EXPLANATIONS

Kfb (Knit Front Back) Knit in to the front and back of the stitch to create an extra stitch.
DblInc (Double Increase) Knit into the front, back, and front of the stitch to create two extra stitches.
Slip slip knit Slip 2 stitches one at a time as if to knit, then knit them together.

BASE

Cast on 10 stitches with B. Divide evenly on double-pointed needles. Place marker and join for working in the round, being careful not to twist.
Round 1 Knit.
Round 2 *(Kfb, knit 1); repeat from * to end of round—15 stitches.
Round 3 Knit 1, *(DblInc, knit 2); repeat from * ending knit 1—25 stitches.
Rounds 4–5 Knit.

Round 6 K2, *(DblInc, knit 4); repeat from * ending knit 2—35 stitches.
Round 7 Knit.
Round 8 K3, *(DblInc, knit 6); repeat from * ending knit 3—45 stitches.
Rounds 9–10 Knit.
Round 11 K4, *(DblInc, knit 8); repeat from * ending knit 4—55 stitches.
Switch to circular needle.
Round 12 Knit.
Round 13 Purl.

STAR POINT—MAKE 5

With B and right (knit) side facing use circular needle and two double-pointed needles.
Row 1 Knit 11 stitches. Leave remaining stitches on circular needle. Turn work.
Row 2 and all wrong side (even) rows Purl.

Row 3 Slip slip knit, knit to last 2 stitches, knit 2 stitches together—9 stitches.

Repeat rows 2 and 3 until 3 stitches remain, ending on wrong side. Place remaining 3 stitches on holder or waste yarn, and break yarn leaving 6" (15 cm) tail. Repeat 4 times.

FLOWER PETAL—MAKE 5

Use double-pointed needles.

With A and right (knit) side facing, working from right to left, pick up 11 stitches in the following manner: 5 stitches down side of star point (use holes from slip slip knit as guide), 1 stitch between star points, 5 stitches up side of star point (use holes from knit 2 stitches together as guide). Turn work. See Figure 1.

Rows 1, 3, and 5 Purl.

Row 2 Knit 1, *(Kfb, knit 1); repeat from *—16 stitches.

Row 4 Slip 1 stitch (B) from holder onto left needle. Knit first 2 stitches on needle together. Knit to last stitch. Slip 1 stitch to right needle. With left needle, pick up 1 stitch (B) from holder. Slip 1 stitch from right needle back to left needle and knit both stitches together.

Row 6 Knit.

Row 7 Purl 8. Position needles for 3-needle bind-off with left needle in back. Bind off until 4 stitches remain on back (left) needle. Slip 1 stitch on third needle to right needle. Purl remaining 4 stitches on left needle—9 stitches.

Row 8 With right needle, pick up 1 stitch where A and B meet. Knit across row. With right needle, pick up 1 stitch where A and B meet—11 stitches.

Row 9 Purl.

Place stitches on holder or waste yarn, and break yarn, leaving 6" (15 cm) tail. (Each holder should contain 1 B stitch and 11 A stitches.)

Repeat four times. On final repeat, do not break yarn. (At the end of this section, each holder should contain 1 B stitch and 11 A stitches.)

CASING—MAKE ONE

Transfer all stitches onto circular needle. Place marker and join for working in the round, being careful not to twist—60 stitches.

Round 1 Knit.

Round 2 Knit 5, *(Sl1, knit 2 stitches together, pass slip stitch over, knit 9) rep from * around, ending knit 4—50 stitches.

Rounds 3, 4 & 5 Knit.

Round 6 *(Knit 2 stitches together, yarn over) rep from * around.

Rounds 7 & 8 Knit.

Bind off.

DRAWSTRING—MAKE 1

Using B and double-pointed needles, cast on 2 stitches.

Work I-cord as follows:

Knit 2 stitches, do not turn.

Slide stitches to opposite end of the needle, carrying yarn in back.

Repeat until I-cord measures 42" (105 cm)

Bind off.

FINISHING

Turn work wrong side out. Pull all loose ends tight before weaving in. Weave in ends. Turn work right-side out.

Weave I-cord drawstring in and out of every other eyelet until all eyelets are used. Bring drawstring out through the first eyelet and knot ends.

LUELLA DISCO PURSE

DESIGNED BY CANDI CANE CANNCEL

KNIT/BEGINNER

Whoever Luella is, she sure has style—take her purse to the disco . . . or anywhere!

SIZE

8" x 6¼" (20 x 15 cm), excluding handles

MATERIALS

 LION BRAND® INCREDIBLE
100% NYLON
1¾ OZ (50 G) 110 YD (100 M) BALL

2 balls #204 Accent on Black, or color of your choice

- Size #10 (6 mm) straight needles
- 2 Darice Craft Designer Silver handles 5½" x 4" (14 x 10 cm) or handles of your choice
- 1 piece of black cotton fabric 9" x 7¼" (22.5 x 18.25 cm) (optional but recommended for lining)
- 20 small clear rhinestones
- Sewing needle
- Tapestry needle
- Black sewing thread
- Aleene Tacky Glue or similar strong glue

GAUGE

20 stitches + 30 rows = 4" (10 cm) in garter stitch.
Gauge is not overly important in this project.

PURSE

Cast on 35 stitches. Knit in garter stitch until piece measures 16" (40 cm). Cast off.

FINISHING

Fold piece in half. Using tapestry needle, sew together the sides using mattress stitch.
Fold lining fabric in half (if using), and stitch up sides.
To attach handles: Cut 4 pieces of Incredible yarn about 2" (5 cm) long. You will be attaching these pieces about 1" (2.5 cm) from sides of each piece to secure the handles. Fold piece in half. Slip folded half through square handle attachment piece and fold over, pin to purse, then stitch to purse. Attach other side of handle. Then attach the next handle in the same manner, making sure that handles line up evenly.

FRINGE

Cut 30 pieces of Incredible 7" (17.5 cm) long (if you like, you may use more or longer pieces). Fold each piece in half and, starting at one bottom end of purse, use tapestry needle to thread fringe piece through from back to front. Pull loose ends through looped end, and pull gently to tighten. Do this all the way across the bottom of the purse to create fringe. Trim so that fringe is even. If you prefer, you may use a crochet hook to pull each piece of fringe through.

For rhinestones: Place a drop of glue where you want the rhinestone and top with rhinestone. Do this 10 times to each side of purse for a total of 20 stones.

POWERBOOK SLEEVE

DESIGNED BY AMY O'NEILL HOUCK
CROCHET/BEGINNER

Even laptops need love! Show yours you care with this cushy padded sleeve.

SIZE

To fit a 12 (15, 17)" (30.5 [38, 43] cm) laptop

MATERIALS

 LION BRAND® LANDSCAPES 50% WOOL, 50% ACRYLIC 1¾ OZ (50 G) 55 YD (50 M) BALL

3 (4, 4) balls #279 Deep Sea

- Size M/N-13 (9 mm) crochet hook, *or size to obtain gauge*
- Large-eyed, blunt needle

GAUGE

9 single crochet + 12 rows = 4" (10 cm).
2 complete shell sequences plus single crochet from next shell + 6 rows of shell pattern = 4" (10 cm). *Be sure to check your gauge.*

BASE

Chain 26 (30, 34).
Round 1 Work 24 (28, 32) single crochet in top loop of each chain. 3 single crochet in top loop of last chain. Do not turn. Continue to single crochet along the back loop of the chain for 23 single crochet. 3 single crochet in last back loop— 54 (58, 62) stitches. Mark the end of the round but do not join. Continue to spiral for all rounds. Work 3 more rounds of single crochet.

BODY OF SLEEVE

Round 1 *(Single crochet in next stitch, 3 double crochet in the following stitch, skip 2 stitches); repeat from * to the end of the round, ending with a single crochet. (Again, do not turn; continue to spiral.)
Round 2 *(3 double crochet in next single crochet , skip 2 double crochet, single crochet in next double crochet) repeat from * around.
Continue to spiral, repeating round 2 until work measures 9 (10, 11)" (22.5 [25, 27.5] cm). Finish current round. Turn.

BEGIN FLAP

Row 1 Chain 3, *(single crochet in next stitch, double crochet in following stitch); repeat from * to the end of the row, ending on a double crochet.
Row 2 Chain 1, *(double crochet in next stitch, single crochet in following stitch); repeat from * to the end of the row, ending with single crochet.
Repeat rows 1 and 2 until flap measures 5" (12.5 cm).
Fasten off. Weave in ends.

7.
HAND JIVE

Keep your hands toasty this winter with an assortment of mittens and wrist warmers. Just a few skeins of yarn can warm up your entire family! The projects in this chapter are so eye-catching, lost mittens will be a thing of the past—no naughty kittens here!

MOLLY MITTENS

DESIGNED BY ANDI SMITH FOR KNITBRIT
KNIT/INTERMEDIATE

Let the colorful yarn do the work for you here—add a fluffy cuff and you've got some stylin' mittens.

SIZE

Women's M
Samples shown Approximately 11" long x 4" wide (28 x 10 cm)

MATERIALS

 LION BRAND® LION® WOOL
100% WOOL
2 OZ (78 G) 143 YD (131 M) BALL

2 balls #203 Ocean Blues (A), or color of your choice

 LION BRAND TIFFANY
100% NYLON
1¾ OZ (50G) 137 YD (125M) SKEIN

1 skein #153 Black (B), or color of your choice

- Size 3 (3.25 mm) double-pointed needles, *or size to obtain gauge*
- Stitch holder
- Large-eyed, blunt needle

GAUGE

16 stitches and 24 rows = 4" (10 cm).
Be sure to check your gauge.

PATTERN NOTE

To get 2 strands of Tiffany from one ball, pull the center thread and the outside thread and use them together.

LEFT MITTEN

CUFF

With 2 strands of B (see Pattern Note), cast on 44 stitches and divide evenly onto 4 needles.
Row 1 Knit.
Row 2 Purl.
Work rows 1 and 2 until piece measures 4" (10 cm) from beginning, decreasing 1 stitch at the beginning of each needle on last row.

HAND

Change to A and work 4 rows of knit 1, purl 1 rib.
Rows 5–12 Knit.

THUMB GUSSET

Row 13 Knit 2, increase 1, knit 1, increase 1, knit to end—12 stitches on needle 1, 10 stitches on other needles.
Row 14 Knit.
Row 15 Knit 2, increase 1, knit 3, increase 1, knit to end—14 stitches on needle 1.
Row 16 Knit.
Row 17 Knit 2, increase 1, knit 5, increase 1, knit to end—16 stitches on needle 1.
Row 18 Knit.
Row 19 Knit 2, increase 1, knit 7, increase 1, knit to end—18 stitches on needle 1.
Row 20 Knit.

Row 21 Knit 2, increase 1, knit 9, increase 1, knit to end—20 stitches on needle 1.

Row 22 Knit.

Row 23 Knit 2, increase 1, knit 11, increase 1, knit to end—22 stitches on needle 1.

Rows 24–27 Knit.

Row 28 Knit 2, slip next 13 stitches onto holder, cast on 1 stitch, knit remaining 8 stitches on needle 1, then knit to end of row.

Knit every row until mitten reaches tip of little finger.

SHAPE MITTEN TOP

Row 1 On needles 1 and 3: Knit 1, slip slip knit, knit to end. On needles 2 and 4: Knit to last 3 stitches, knit 2 stitches together, knit 1.

Rows 2–3 Knit.

Rows 4–6 Repeat rows 1–3.

Row 7 Knit.

Row 8 On needles 1 and 4: Knit. On needle 2: Knit to last 3 stitches, knit 2 together, knit 1. On needle 3: Knit 1, slip slip knit, knit to end.

Row 9 Knit.

Row 10 Repeat row 8.

Row 11 Repeat row 9.

Row 12 Repeat row 1.

Row 13 Repeat row 9.

Rows 14–17 Repeat rows 10–13.

Bind off. Turn inside out and sew seam.

THUMB

Pick up stitches on holder and 5 stitches along opening at base of thumb and divide among 3 needles—18 stitches.

Knit until thumb reaches about halfway up the thumbnail (approximately 1¾" [4.5 cm]).

Next row Knit 2 stitches together, repeat to end— 9 stitches.

Knit 3 rows. Break yarn and thread through stitches. Pull tightly and fasten off.

RIGHT MITTEN

Work same as for left mitten, except increases for the thumb gusset are worked on needle 4 instead of needle 1.

MAINE MITTENS

DESIGNED BY KATY WESTCOTT

CROCHET/BEGINNER

These dense mittens will keep your hands warm on even the coldest day!

SIZE

Small (Large)

Width 4 (4½)" [11 (12) cm]

Length 9 (11)" [23.5 (29) cm]

MATERIALS

 LION BRAND® LION® WOOL

100% WOOL

3 OZ (85 G) 158 YD (144 M) BALL

1 (2) balls #125 Cocoa (A) and
1 ball #132 Lemongrass (B), or
colors of your choice

- Size E-4 (3.5 mm) crochet hook,
  or size to obtain gauge
- Large-eyed, blunt needle

GAUGE

20 single crochet + 22 rows = 4"
(10 cm).
Be sure to check your gauge.

NOTES

Worked in the round, the mittens

are tightly crocheted with a small
hook to be dense and warm.
Rounds are not joined, but are
worked in a spiral. Place a marker
in the first stitch of the second
round to mark the beginning of the
round. Remove the marker when
working the first single crochet of
each round, and replace it immediately into the stitch you just made.
To change colors, complete the last
stitch, drop the first color to the
inside and draw the second color
through the loop on the hook.
Tighten the first color around the
second, and continue crocheting
as usual.

LEFT MITTEN

Beginning with cuff and A,
chain 30 (35). Join with slip stitch
to form ring.

Round 1 Chain 1, single crochet in
each chain around—30 (35) single
crochet.

Rounds 2–11 (2–13) Single crochet
in each single crochet around.

Round 12 (14) *Single crochet in
each of next 4 single crochet, 2
single crochet in next single
crochet; repeat from * around—36
(42) single crochet.

Round 13 (15) *Single crochet in
each of next 5 (6) single crochet,
2 single crochet in next single
crochet; repeat from * around—42
(48) single crochet.

Rounds 14–24 (16–26) Continue in
single crochet working in the
following color sequence, 5 rounds
B, 2 rounds A, 4 rounds B.

Round 25 (27) *Thumbhole row* With
A, single crochet in each of next 32
(37) single crochet, loosely chain 5
(6), skip 8 (9) single crochet and
single crochet in each of next 2
single crochet.

Round 26 (28) Single crochet in
each single crochet and chain
stitch around.

single crochet until mitten top is closed. Fasten off.

THUMB

With A, attach yarn in any skipped stitch of thumbhole.

Rounds 1–11 (1–15) Working in each single crochet and remaining loop of each chain stitch, single crochet in each stitch around—13 (15) single crochet.

Next Working in one continuous round, single crochet in every other single crochet until thumb is closed. Fasten off. Using large-eyed, blunt needle, weave in ends.

RIGHT MITTEN

Work as for left mitten to round 25.

Round 25 (27) *Thumbhole row*

Single crochet in each of next 2 single crochet, loosely chain 5 (6), skip 8 (9) single crochet, single crochet in each of next 32 (37) single crochet.

Continue with left mitten directions beginning with round 26.

Rounds 27–43 (29–49) Continue in single crochet working the following color sequence, 4 rounds B, 2 rounds A, 4 rounds B, 7 (11) rounds A.

Fasten off B.

Round 44 (50) *With A, single crochet in each of next 5 single crochet, skip next single crochet; repeat from * around—35 (40) single crochet.

Round 45 (51) Single crochet in each single crochet around.

Round 46 (52) *Single crochet in each of next 6 (7) single crochet, skip next single crochet; repeat from * around—30 (35) single crochet.

Rounds 47–50 (53–58) Single crochet in each single crochet around.

Next Working in one continuous round, single crochet in every other

DIAMOND SPIKE STITCH MITTENS

DESIGNED BY KATY WESTCOTT

CROCHET/EXPERIENCED

These colorful mittens are a great small project to test out stitch patterns like the spike stitch seen here.

SIZE

Width 4" (10 cm)
Length 9¼" (23.5 cm)

MATERIALS

 LION BRAND® LION® WOOL
100% WOOL
3 OZ (85 G) 158 YD (144 M) BALL

1 ball each #147 Purple (A), #187 Goldenrod (B), and #132 Lemongrass (C), or colors of your choice

- Size I-9 (5.5 mm) crochet hook, *or size to obtain gauge*
- Large-eyed, blunt needle

GAUGE

5 spike clusters wide and 6 spike clusters tall = 3" (7.5 cm).
Be sure to check your gauge.

STITCH EXPLANATIONS

A single crochet spike stitch is a single crochet that is worked in the top of a stitch 2 or more rows below the working row and drawn up to the height of the new row. This pattern includes two types of spike stitch clusters:

Spike Stitch Cluster Skip 2 single crochet, make 4 single crochet spike stitches all in the same stitch 2 rows below the working round, skip 2 single crochet.

Half-Spike Stitch Cluster Make 2 single crochet spike stitches all in the same stitch 2 rows below the working round, skip 2 single crochet.

LEFT MITTEN

Beginning with cuff and A, chain 20. Join with slip stitch to form ring.

Round 1 Chain 1, single crochet in each chain around. Join with slip stitch in first single crochet—20 single crochet.

Rounds 2–8 Chain 1, single crochet in each single crochet around. Join with slip stitch in first single crochet.

Round 9 Chain 1, 2 single crochet in first single crochet, single crochet in each of next 3 single crochet, *2 single crochet in next single crochet, single crochet in each of next 3 single crochet; repeat from * around. Join with slip stitch in first single crochet—25 single crochet.

Round 10 Chain 1, 2 single crochet in first single crochet, single crochet in each of next 3 single crochet, *2 single crochet in next single crochet, single crochet in each of next 3 single crochet;

repeat from * around, ending 2 single crochet in last single crochet. Join with slip stitch in first single crochet—32 single crochet. Fasten off.

Round 11 With B, chain 1, half spike stitch cluster in top of stitch 2 rounds below, work 7 spike stitch clusters around, half spike stitch cluster in same space as first half spike stitch cluster. Join with slip stitch in first spike stitch—7 spike stitch clusters + 2 half spike stitch clusters.

Round 12 Chain 1, single crochet in each spike stitch around. Join with slip stitch in first spike stitch—32 single crochet.

Round 13 Chain 1, single crochet in each single crochet around. Join with slip stitch in first single crochet. Fasten off.

Round 14 With C, chain 1, work first spike stitch cluster in the center stitch of the triangle space between first 2 spike stitch clusters from round 11, (spike stitch cluster in center stitch of each triangle space around) 7 times. Join with slip stitch in first spike stitch—8 spike stitch clusters.

Round 15 Repeat round 12.

Round 16 Repeat round 13.

Round 17 *Thumbhole row* With A, work 1 half-spike stitch cluster, loosely chain 4, skip next triangle space, work 6 spike stitch clusters around, half-spike stitch cluster in same space as first half-spike stitch cluster. Join with slip stitch in first spike stitch.

Round 18 Chain 1, work 1 single crochet in each spike stitch, and chain stitch around. Join with slip stitch in first single crochet.

Round 19 Repeat round 13.

Round 20 With B, work 2 spike stitch clusters into thumbhole loop, work 6 spike stitch clusters in established pattern around. Join with slip stitch in first spike stitch.

Round 21 Repeat round 12.

Round 22 Repeat round 13.

Rounds 23–46 Repeat rounds 11–16, working 3 rows in each color using the following color sequence: C, A, B, C, A, B, C, A.

Round 47 Chain 1, skip first single crochet, single crochet in each of next 3 single crochet, *skip next single crochet, single crochet in each of next 3 single crochet; repeat from * around. Join with slip stitch in first single crochet—24

single crochet.

Round 48 Repeat round 47—18 single crochet.

Rounds 49–51 Chain 1, single crochet in each single crochet around. Join with slip stitch in first single crochet.

Round 52 Make 1 single crochet in every other single crochet until mitten top is closed. Fasten off. Using large-eyed, blunt needle, weave in ends.

RIGHT MITTEN

Rounds 1–16 Work as for left mitten.

Round 17 *Thumbhole row* With A, work 1 half spike stitch cluster, work 6 spike stitch clusters around to last 2 triangle spaces, loosely chain 4, skip next space, 1 half spike stitch cluster.

Rounds 18–52 Work as for left mitten.

LEFT THUMB

With A, attach yarn in outer edge of thumbhole.

Row 1 Chain 1, single crochet in same stitch, skip next spike stitch cluster, work 3 single crochet in next triangle space, skip next spike

stitch cluster, single crochet in thumbhole stitch at inner edge of mitten, single crochet in first stitch of bottom row, single crochet in next stitch, spike stitch cluster in next stitch, single crochet in last stitch. Join with slip stitch in first single crochet—12 stitches.

Row 2 Chain 1, single crochet in each spike stitch and single crochet around. Join with slip stitch in first single crochet—12 single crochet.

Rows 3–11 Chain 1, single crochet in each single crochet around. Join with slip stitch in first single crochet.

Next Chain 1, single crochet in every other single crochet until thumb is closed.

RIGHT THUMB

With A, join yarn in outer edge of thumbhole.

Round 1 Chain 1, single crochet in first stitch, work 1 spike stitch cluster, single crochet in next stitch, single crochet in thumbhole stitch at inner edge of mitten, single crochet in top of thumbhole, skip next spike stitch cluster, work 3 single crochet in between spike stitch clusters, skip next spike stitch cluster, single crochet in last stitch. Join with slip stitch in first single crochet—12 stitches.

Round 2 Chain 1, work single crochet in each single crochet and spike stitch around. Join with slip stitch in first single crochet—12 single crochet.

Rounds 3–11 Chain 1, single crochet in each single crochet around. Join with slip stitch in first single crochet.

Next Chain 1, single crochet in every other single crochet until thumb is closed. Fasten off.

FINISHING

Using large-eyed, blunt needle, weave in ends.

LITTLE BITS MITTS

DESIGNED BY AMY POPE

KNIT/EASY

These mitts were originally invented to use up my first few small skeins of handspun, but I knew I wouldn't have enough to make two whole mitts. A ball of plain worsted lying nearby was the solution. These mitts are thick and warm but leave the fingers and thumb free to manipulate keys and buttons. They can also be worn with a set of gloves underneath for extra warmth. Using paired increases creates a symmetrical edge to the thumb gusset, and these yarn over increases are easier to work in bulky yarns than picking up the bar between stitches.

SIZE

Woman's M/L
Sample shown Approximately 8" long x 3½" wide (20 x 8.8 cm)

MATERIALS

 LION BRAND® LANDSCAPES 50% WOOL 50% ACRYLIC
1¾ OZ (50 G) 55 YD (50 M) BALL

1 ball #277 Country Sunset (A)

LION BRAND® LION® WOOL 100% WOOL
3 OZ (85 G) 158 YD (144 M) BALL

1 ball #178 Deep Teal (B)
- Set of 5 double-pointed needles in size 9 (5.5 mm), *or size to obtain gauge*
- Large-eyed, blunt needle

GAUGE

A: 13 stitches + 20 rows = 4" (10 cm).
B: 14.5 stitches + 22 rows = 4" (10 cm).
Be sure to check your gauge.

STITCH EXPLANATIONS

M1R (Make 1 Right) Yarn over backward, and when knitting the yarn over, knitting it through the front leg of the stitch.

M1L (Make 1 Left) Yarn over normally, and when knitting the yarn over on the subsequent row, knit through the back leg of the stitch.

CUFF

Cast on 20 stitches with A. Join, being careful not to twist, and place marker to indicate beginning of round. Work in knit 2, purl 2 rib for 12 rounds. On round 13, begin

knitting in stockinette stitch (knit every round). Work in stockinette stitch for 3 rounds. At beg of next round, M1L and place marker. You will now have one new stitch between the round beginning marker and the new marker. This stitch is the beginning of the thumb gusset.

GUSSET

Knit 1 round even, then slip marker, M1R, knit 1, M1L. Knit 2 rounds even, and then work the gusset as follows:

Round 1 Slip marker, M1R, knit to marker, M1L, slip marker, knit remainder of round in stockinette stitch—2 stitches increased.

Rounds 2–4 Knit.

Repeat these 4 rounds twice (8 rounds total), then break yarn and change to B. On first round of B, increase 3 stitches evenly around.

Resume working 4-round gusset increase pattern in B until you have 13 stitches between the gusset markers. (Make sure to knit rounds 2–4 after your final increase row.) Place all gusset stitches between markers on a piece of scrap yarn. These will be picked up later to knit the thumb ribbing.

Continue knitting on the hand stitches. Knit around from the gusset, casting on 1 stitch over the gap formed by the removal of the thumb stitches—24 stitches. Knit 4 rounds, then break yarn and begin knitting with A. Knit 2 rounds stockinette, and then work 6 rounds in knit 2, purl 2 rib. Bind off in pattern.

THUMB

Remove thumb stitches from waste yarn and place on double-pointed needles.

Round 1 Knit, picking up 2 stitches over the gap where the thumb joins the hand. Place marker between these 2 picked-up stitches to indicate beginning of round.

Round 2 Knit to last 2 stitches, knit 2 stitches together.

Round 3 Slip slip knit, knit to end of round.

Round 4 Purl 2 stitches together, purl 1, *knit 2, purl 2; repeat from * to end of round.

Continue to knit in knit 2, purl 2 rib for 6 rows. Bind off in rib pattern.

FINISHING

Weave in all ends, using yarn tails to neaten any gaps that may remain at the junction between the thumb and hand. Wash and block.

YARN INDEX

AIRLINE PILLOW, PAGE 75

BLUE BANANA DISHCLOTH, PAGE 35

BOBBLETTE DISHCLOTH, PAGE 33

BRAIDED SHORTIE SCARF, PAGE 26

CAT SUSHI, PAGE 51

CORNMEAL CABLE DISHCLOTH, PAGE 38

CROCHET CAT BED, PAGE 83

DECORATIVE COLLAR, PAGE 60

DIAMOND SPIKE STITCH MITTENS, PAGE 103

FELTED NEWSBOY HAT, PAGE 79

FORGET-ME-NOT TEDDY BEAR HAT AND SHOE SET, PAGE 23

GIRL'S BOLERO, PAGE 20

GLITTERSPUN GIFT BAG, PAGE 86

GREEK KEY COFFEE COZIES, PAGE 72

HOLIDAY ORNAMENTS AND GIFT TAGS, PAGE 47

HOLLY DOG SWEATER, PAGE 57

LITTLE BITS MITTS, PAGE 107

LUELLA DISCO PURSE, PAGE 92

MAINE MITTENS, PAGE 100

MOLLY MITTENS, PAGE 97

POWERBOOK SLEEVE, PAGE 95

PROVENÇAL AFGHAN, PAGE 41

SCOTT THE BEAR, PAGE 15

SOLAR SYSTEM NECKLACE, PAGE 63

SOPHIE DOG SWEATER, PAGE 54

SPARKLY ANKLE BRACELETS, PAGE 66

STARFLOWER SATCHEL, PAGE 88

THROW PILLOW, PAGE 29

INDEX